FRONT COVER

The objects pictured on the front cover represent key elements and characters in the story—the Ojibwe Circle of Life, the Georgia peanuts, the Union Cavalryman's Civil War cap and belt buckle. The tall trees symbolize the forest that was cut to build the stockade at Anderson Station, Georgia which became the infamous Andersonville Confederate Prison, during the height of the U. S. Civil War.

The front cover is by photographer, Rebecca Hutchinson Crum and artist/designer, Janelle Henley Whetstone, who is a member of the Lac Courte Oreilles band of Wisconsin Ojibwe.

ACKNOWLEDGEMENTS

My sincere appreciation goes to those librarians, teachers and students who read the manuscript and offered valuable comments and suggestions for improving the story: Luann W. Hodges; Mari W. Newton; Steve McClendon; Michael Melton; Katie Jane Morris; Janet W. Seaman; Dr. Shirley Spears; Judy Tidwell and the countless young Alabama students who listened to readings from Joe's story and responded with intriguing questions and surprising insight. Thanks also to the staff at the Andersonville National Historic Site for help and support with this project. A special thanks to Janelle Whetstone for her patient editing and guidance into the Objibwe culture of her ancestry.

DEDICATION

This book is dedicated to the memory of Pvt. François H. Beauregard and all the other prisoners of war who died unidentified, in the service of their country.

François H. Beauregard joined the Wisconsin Vounteers, Co. A, 7th Regiment, in January 1864 to fight with the Union Army, in the Civil War. He was wounded and captured by Confederate soldiers in May at The Battle of the Wilderness in Virginia and sent to a prison near Andersonville, Georgia where he is reported to have died in September. After the war ended Clara Barton led a U. S. Government delegation to this prison site to identify approximately 13,000 Union prisoners of war who had died there and to erect proper markers for their graves. Pvt. Beauregard's body was among the over four hundred Nurse Barton failed to identify. Did François H. Beauregard actually die in that horrendous stockade at Camp Sumter, later known as Andersonville Prison, or was he among the many that faked death and escaped into the darkness? Joe's story is one response to this question; however, *Goober Joe* is a work of fiction and not to be construed as factual.

GOOBER JOE
Coming of Age ~ A Civil War Novel

By

Bob Whetstone

Lulu.com

*"I dream I turn into a hawk, a red tail hawk
with a sharp beak. I fly off to the camp to
peck out the eyes o' all the kids that ever
made fun o' me. As I fly over the stockade
another hawk digs outta the grave ditch 'n
flys 'long with me. He says, 'Where you
goin' Goober Hawk?' I tell 'im what I
wanna do to the camp kids. He says, 'Won't
do no good.' I ask 'im why and he says,
'They'll see you the same way, even with
their eyes put out.' I ask 'im how he knows
so much. He says, **'The higher you fly, the
more you see.'** Then he takes off flyin' to
the sun."*

ISBN 978-0-615-25761-7

1

The awful smell o' the prison takes my breath long 'fore I
see guards standin' in their pigeon roosts on the stockade wall.
These August dog days make the stench worse'n Massa Carter's
hog pen 'n it carries all the way past the railroad depot. I hate
goin' to that stinkin' prison camp, but I gotta haul my peanuts over
there if I want the guards to buy 'em. It ain't the guards that smell
bad; it's the bluecoat Yankees in the stockade. They smell like
they're dyin'. Most are. I see 'em gittin' dumped off flat bed
wagons into grave pits like piles o' bones. I ain't s'posed to git
close 'nough to see their faces. That's all right with me. All Ben
'n me want is to peddle my peanuts; then git back to the farm like a
fox on the run.

"Ain't that right, Ben?"

Ben 'n me been comin' to the prison camp ever since General
Lee sent the first bluecoat prisoners here last winter. Mr. Dukes,
the camp sutler, put Momma 'n me in bi'ness haulin' goods from
the farm—sweet potatoes, corn, onions, peas 'n peanuts. Momma
sends me 'n Ben over to the camp to sell roasted peanuts. When
my croaker sack's empty, I head back to the farm with a pocket
full o' tokens. If I'm lucky, a guard'll give me a Union two-cent
token I can swap for more Confed money.

"Come on Ben, I see the stockade wall pokin' up over the
grave ditches."

Talkin' to a donkey might seem strange to some folk, but ain't nobody else to talk to 'cept Momma 'n Tater. Momma won't let Tater come with me. She says the bluecoats are so hungry they skin 'n eat dogs that come too close to the stockade. Momma's 'fraid the guards' bloodhounds'll pick a fight with Tater.

"Know what I think, Ben? I think she don't wanna be by herself while I'm tradin' peanuts."

Like all the folk 'round these parts, Momma's 'fraid o' bluecoats breakin' out 'n hidin' 'round the farm. Every time a prisoner gets loose, guards come to the farm lookin' for the poor devil.

Corporal Tolliver's voice still rings in my ears like a squeaky barn door. "Della, if we catch Feds hidin' out on this property, we'll throw you 'n yo' boy in the stockade with the rest o' the traitors." He ain't much more'n jist a pup, but that gun he totes makes 'im stand tall…'n mean.

"C'mon Ben, quit kickin' up so much dust."

This time 'o year Oglethorpe Road ain't nothin' but red dust 'til it rains, then it turns slick as boiled okra. I move to the other side of Ben to put him 'n the cart he's pullin' 'tween me 'n the Confederate graveyard b'side the road. Ghosts don't scare me none in daylight; I jist like to walk fast past buryin' grounds.

On down the road, my skin gets tight. T'other side o' the railroad track's the pine thicket that slaves left standin' for firewood when they built the stockade. Both sides o' the road are so thick with trees a prisoner could jump on me quicker'n a flea hops on a dog. I pop Ben on the rump with my hand.

"Giddy-up Ben, gotta git through heah 'fore we meet up with trouble."

I pull on the cart helpin' Ben guide the wheels through the hard ruts. My heart's poundin' in my chest like a drum, 'til we reach the clearin' by Stockade Creek. I hold my nose 'n lead Ben through the shallow brown water runnin' out o' the stockade.

"Hidee, Goober boy."

Uh oh, Corporal Tolliver's hollerin' at me. I hate that sorry excuse for a soldier, mainly 'cause he calls me "Goober," a name I hate more'n snakes. Now most o' the guards call me "Goober Joe." Thought I'd git used to it, but it rubs me raw. Somebody oughta gimme a better name than "Goober" to go with Joe.

"I see you made it through the robbers' cove. See any one-eyed Yankees with long knives? You're lucky. I heah they just love to eat little slave boys with light skin like yo'rn."

Pretendin' he ain't talkin' to me, I tuck my head 'n pull Ben on towards the carpenter shop. The corporal's wild stories don't scare me none. Paroled bluecoat prisoners work 'round camp like regular folk.

"I see you got a sack full o' goobers."

The corporal wants some peanuts in trade for protection from Union prisoners, but he's the only one that bothers me.

"I'll jist help myself to some goobers, boy." Corporal Tolliver reaches to untie the croaker sack in the cart.

I whack Ben on the rump 'n we run on past the surprised guard. Another guard stops us as the corporal catches up.

"Got goobers, Joe?"

"Yessuh, for a penny token."

Corporal Tolliver stands back to let me loosen the string to fish out a double handful o' peanuts 'n drop 'em in the guard's hat. He flips me a token 'n stares at Corporal Tolliver who stands 'round grinnin' like he's gonna git some. The guard puts the peanuts in his pocket 'n walks 'long with me 'n Ben a ways, crackin' 'n flippin' goobers in 'is mouth.

I hurry on down to Mr. Dukes' store where Momma trades goods. He comes outta the store totin' a sack o' feed 'n takes notice o' me.

"Hidee, Joe."

He don't call me "Goober" 'n I 'preciate that. Mr. Dukes sets the sack down 'n squints his eyes at the corporal.

"Tolliver, you been bothering this boy again?"

The corporal backs up 'n grins.

"No suh, I'm jist waitin' for the peanuts I bought."

Mr. Dukes cocks his head like he don't believe 'im. Corporal Tolliver takes off his hat 'n pushes it towards me.

"Is that right, Joe?" Mr. Dukes wants to know. I don't say nothin'. "Tolliver if you're lying…"

"No suh, I swear I ain't lyin'. He put my token right there in his pocket. Take it out boy, 'n show 'im."

I know he's lyin', he knows he's lyin', but Mr. Dukes don't know he's lyin'. I can't win this fuss 'tween white folk, so I untie the string 'n give 'im the peanuts he ain't paid for. He goes on back towards the creek shellin' 'n eatin' his free goobers.

"One day you'll be big enough to pop that weasel up side the head, Joe, and I reckon I'll just turn my back and won't see a thing."

The sutler comes off the porch for his peanuts 'n hands me a token. I tie Ben to the post at the end o' the porch 'n wait for more Georgia Reserves to come with their money. Mr. Dukes likes my peanuts 'n he treats me real nice. There's 'nother sutler store inside the stockade, but Mr. Dukes's the only one Momma 'n the farmers 'round here trade with. I ain't 'llowed any closer'n this to the gate.

BAM!

A rifle shot from the stockade sends me jumpin' nearly into next week.

"Hallelujah! Another sorry bluecoat crossed the dead line and went on to glory," a guard hollers from the porch behind me. He laughs—like it's funny to kill a man.

"How 'bout some goobers, boy."

The shot still rings in my head as I dig out the guard's peanuts. Gunshots ain't new to me, but I don't know 'xactly why a guard takes a notion to shoot a prisoner that can't shoot back. Momma told me to never ask questions 'bout the camp, so I keep my mouth shut 'n give the guard his peanuts. But there's a lot that goes on she don't know 'bout. Like when Capt'n Wirtz hollers at Mr. Dukes on 'is way to the stockade.

"Red, do we have enough provisions to feed four hundred more Yankees coming in today?"

Mr. Red Dukes shakes 'is head 'n laughs, "Four hundred, four thousand, don't make much difference. I'll water down the cornbread and slice the bacon thinner." Capt'n Wirtz growls and stomps off.

The old man guardin' the store asks, "What's the Old Dutchman got stuck in his craw?"

Mr. Dukes shakes 'is head. "Same ol' story, I reckon; too many prisoners, not enough food."

Mr. Dukes hollers, "Joe, come over here." Then he squats down 'n gives me orders, "When you're done here go tell your momma to bring over a load of provisions tomorrow."

"Yessuh."

"Good boy. Has she heard from Major Carter lately?" I shake my head. "Good man, that Major Carter, a real soldier of the Confederacy." Then he whispers, "Not like some of these sapling reserve guards around here."

Yeah, Massa Carter's a real soldier all right. I 'member the day he got a letter after the war started. He gathered Momma 'n the field hands 'round the veranda o' the big house. "Y'all listen," he said, wavin' the paper in 'is hand. "This here's my commission from General Robert E. Lee himself. I am now Major Carter, Army of the Confederate States of America. Della, you help Mrs. Carter make my uniform. While I'm gone, y'all take care of the place and gather the crops. The Yankees don't have the guts for fighting a real war, so I'll be back home soon."

Two weeks later, I helped Massa Carter saddle his black stallion in the barn.

"Now, Joe, you help take care of this place and don't fuss with my girls." I heard 'im talkin', but 'is jinglin' spurs 'n sword smackin' 'gainst 'is fresh gray britches conjured up thoughts o' fightin' 'stead o' plowin'.

"You heah me, Joe?"

"Oh, yessuh."

He led 'is horse to the front yard where Missy Carter waited with her two little girls 'n Momma. Everybody was cryin' 'cept me 'n Massa Carter. He stood tall, 'is brass buttons shinin' 'n the pearl handle on 'is pistol catchin' the sun. I hankered to see 'im snatch the sword outta its scabbard jist one time 'fore he climbed up on the stallion.

"I wanna go too," I hollered without thinkin'.

Massa Carter laughed, "I could use a drummer boy, but I need a man around here to take care of the womenfolk."

Then he turned to Momma 'n told 'er to see after Missy Carter 'n the kids. He mounted his black stallion 'n rode off with leather squeakin' 'n spurs a'jinglin'. I ain't seen 'im since.

'Fore she moved to Macon, Missy Carter used to get letters. She'd sit on the veranda cryin' 'n readin' the letters to 'er chillun.

'T'wan't long 'til the field hands ran off leavin' nobody 'cept Momma 'n me to help with the harvest. Missy Carter went 'round Anderson Station beggin' folks to help us bring in the crops.

"Anythin' to help the Major's family," they said, even though most of 'em were old people 'n half-growed chillun. But when they didn't show up for spring plantin' Missy Carter cut back 'n put in jist 'nough potatoes, corn, peas 'n onions to last through winter. I saved the peanut patch for myself, not knowin' then what I'd do with more'n we could eat.

When we got word that General Lee would build a prison for captured Union soldiers at Camp Sumter, everythin' changed, like when it comes up a cloud on a clear day.

"I will not raise my children near a prison camp," Missy Carter declared. Soon, her daddy 'n another man came over in a wagon 'n hauled the whole bunch back to Macon. She told Momma, "Della, you take care of the plantation until we come back." That was last winter 'n we ain't seen 'er since.

Ever since Missy Carter left, Momma calls where we live a *farm*. "This place ain't a plantation no more'n I'm a white lady," she says.

Even though the prison at Camp Sumter was too close to Anderson Station for Missy Carter, it's makin' a livin' for Momma 'n me. I got in the peanut b'iness when Momma let me use 'er wash pot to boil 'n roast raw peanuts over hickory coals. I'll pull up a new crop this fall 'n boil 'em green, with salt. Everybody likes boiled peanuts. What's left over I'll hang up in the barn to dry for roastin' in winter.

There's a lot I wanna know 'bout the prison, but don't ask for fear Captain Wirtz'll kick me outta camp like that gambler 'n his tap-dancin' lady friend. Momma ain't much help either.

"Mercy, it ain't our place to understand, jist bear our burdens 'n trust the Lord," she says. But her way o' thinkin' don't kill my wonderin' ways.

I sell peanuts by the store 'til the August sun bears down hotter'n the devil's breath. Sometimes there's some left over, but today tradin' was good. I throw the empty sack in the cart 'n lead Ben over to the water trough. A far away train-whistle stirs up the camp. The Georgia Reserves pour out o' their tents wavin' their rifles 'n headin' to the depot. Traders 'n women folk follow close b'hind.

I'm s'posed to leave camp 'fore the train comes in, but today I take a notion to see bluecoats comin' into the camp fresh from fightin' and gittin' captured. Nobody notices me, so I wander over to the storehouse next to the depot 'n tie Ben to a crate. Then I climb up a stack o' crates, takin' my empty croaker sack to keep from fryin' my hands on the hot roof.

The Georgia reserves herd the bluecoats out o' the cattle cars callin' 'em "fresh fish, fresh fish," 'n pullin' at their b'longin's tryin' to take their coats, hats 'n bundles.

"Y'all let'em keep their hats; there ain't no shade in the compound," a sergeant hollers.

The scraggly men in dirty blue uniforms are a pitiful lot. From the roof I can see inside the stockade for the first time. There ain't nothin' but little tents 'n sheds, with men millin' 'round pine stumps spread all over the slope. The new prisoners wander into the stockade 'n head to the creek to pee. I slip back off the roof, 'fraid o' gittin' caught spyin'.

While people in the camp watch prisoners unload 'n go in the stockade, Ben 'n me head out Oglethorpe Road. We wait at the creek hopin' somebody'll come by 'n let us go with 'em through the spooky stretch o' woods ahead. A man I know from Anderson Station leaves the camp, so Ben 'n me follow his wagon through the thicket 'n 'cross the railroad track.

When we come to the rise overlookin' the death trenches, a strange site makes me stop dead in my tracks. Four men in ragged blue britches 'n filthy shirts carry a body slung in a blanket. A confederate guard stands a good ways back hollerin'. The guard sees me 'n Ben 'n waves us on down the road. I stop behind some scrub brush, tie Ben to a bush 'n sneak up close to watch.

The four men move on past the death trenches 'n close to the road 'fore the guard lowers his gun 'n hollers, "Ho, far enough!" I thought he'd shoot, but he jist stands there watchin'.

Two men take shovels from the blanket 'n start diggin'. The other two pull back small piles o' red dirt with their hands. The men in the hole do somethin' odd. They squat down actin' like they're diggin' 'til the guard turns his back. Then they slip the body in the grave, cover it with pine branches 'n scatter a little dirt over the limbs. As the buryin' crew walks back to the stockade, the guard follows way b'hind like he's 'fraid of 'em.

Yankees sure are lazy—too lazy to bury their dead in a proper grave. Won't be long 'fore the buzzards home in on their buddy 'n pick at 'is bones.

Ben brays loud to let me know he's tired o' waitin'. I scoot through the brush, not lookin' back to see if the guard's gonna shoot me.

"Just for that, stupid donkey, you can pull me back to the Carter place. You could a' got me shot 'n then where'd you be? You'd stay hitched to this wagon the rest o' yo' life 'cause nobody'd give a hoot 'bout a donkey that don't know when to keep 'is mouth shut." After fussin' at Ben, I squeeze inside my cart 'n slack off on the reins.

"Let's git on, Ben, I gotta slop the hogs, put up livestock 'n do the milkin' 'fore supper."

2

Little clouds o' red dust boil up from the cart's wheels makin' Ben snort 'n me sneeze on our way back to the farm. I hope for rain to settle the dust, but this part o' Georgia don't get much this time o' year. Hot weather's better for cotton 'n peanuts than for boys 'n donkeys. Ben gets tired 'n slows down. My legs cramp, so I get out 'n walk the rest o' the way. We turn off the main road 'tween two split rail corners that mark the wagon trail to the main house. It used to be a fence, but somebody too lazy to cut firewood stole most o' the rails last winter. The place growed up since the war started, but I keep the wagon trail clear o' weeds best I can. Wouldn't want Ben to come up on a snake 'n scare us both half to death. Ben pokes b'hind me through the line o' shady oak trees leadin' to the big house. I hear barkin' way in the distance.

"Hey Ben, I wonder what Tater's after." The closer we get, the louder the barkin', but that dog's still a long way off. Ben lets out a short bray to let Momma know we're comin'. He knows he'll be chompin' on corn 'fore long. We go 'round Massa Carters' house towards the barn.

"Put up the donkey 'n hurry over here, Joe," Momma hollers from the cabin porch, keepin' 'er eyes on the cornfield.

She sounds worried, so I trot Ben d'rectly to the barn, unhitch him 'n promise to feed 'n water 'im after I see what's botherin' Momma. I run over 'n hop up on the porch to have a look.

"That hound's been carryin' on like that for a while. Somethin's out there Joe." Momma's white eyeballs get wider as she talks, like the time she come up on a copperhead while cuttin' broom straw.

"Tater's just treed a 'possum 'n wants me to come shake it down." I try to sound braver 'n I feel.

"Not in daylight, Joe. He ain't barkin' up no tree. Listen, that hound's mad at what he's got cornered." I put my arm 'round Momma to settle 'er down 'n somethin' hard bangs 'gainst my hand.

"Momma!"

She pulls the double-barreled gun 'way from where she's hidin' it in the folds of 'er dress 'n hands it to me.

"It ain't loaded yet. I don't know where Massa Carter keeps 'is shells." I back off from the gun. "Here, take it, Joe. I know Massa Carter took you out 'n taught you to shoot. It wan't no big secret."

If Momma'd slapped me down, I wouldn't o' been more surprised. 'Fore Massa Carter left for the army, he took me to the woods with his shotgun. The first time I pulled the trigger, it knocked me on my butt. He helped me up, showed me how to brace for the kick 'n let me shoot 'til I splattered a pine saplin' with buckshot. I remember he said, *You'll be the man of the house, Joe. If a stray Yankee comes around Mrs. Carter and my girls, don't you be afraid to cut him down like that sapling. You can pass for a white boy easily, Joe, so be strong and stand your ground.* I can't 'magine passin' for a white boy 'cause people in these parts know my momma's a slave. She ain't dark as night, but she's still Massa Carter's slave.

"Reckon Tater's got a bluecoat cornered, Momma?"

"Find the shells, Joe 'n let's go 'n see."

I nearly swallow my tongue tryin' hard not to let Momma see me scared. I prop the gun 'gainst the rail, run over to the big house 'n slip through the cellar door, leavin' it open to light my way to the stair steps. The cool cellar air feels good on my face, but I don't stop 'til my fingers feel the latch on the kitchen door. The door creaks open to the dark room that smells like a cave. My eyes wander 'round 'til it lightens up enough to find my way to Massa Carter's library. I crawl under his desk 'n run my hand 'cross the side panel feelin' for the knob that pops open the drawers. Scootin' from under the desk, I pull open the bottom drawer 'n lift out a box o' shotgun shells. Massa Carter's warnin' rattles 'round in my head. *Be careful not to knock the shells together, they might go off in your hands.* I pick out two shells; put the box back in the drawer 'n back track through the kitchen 'n cellar like I'm totin' eggs.

The cellar door slams b'hind me 'n sets my teeth on edge.

Momma hollers, "Come on, Joe, Tater's bark's gittin' weak." She hands me the shotgun. I break it open 'n slide the shells in, one at a time.

She grabs the wash pot paddle for her weapon. "You go first. I don't want that gun to go off 'n rip off my backside."

"Yessum."

I take off through the peanut patch to the cornfield. The tall brownin' stalks hide us 'til we come to bare ground where we ran out o' seed last spring. Once we come out o' the cornfield, Tater's barkin' gets louder.

"He's over yonder in the hollow by the creek."

"Shush, Joe; don't holler."

Momma's right, Tater's bark sounds funny, like the time he tangled with a bear. My scalp gets tight, but I can't let on I'm scared. We come to the edge o' the gum stand close to the creek. I slow down 'n point the gun towards the trees.

"We're real close," I whisper to Momma.

Tater hears us comin'. He yelps to let us know where he's at.

"Tater, come 'ere, boy."

He stops barkin' 'n then starts up again. I cock one barrel 'n move forward. We come over the rise 'n look down to the creek.

"Tater!" My redbone hound turns 'is head 'n looks up at me, but stands 'is ground like a bloodhound.

"He's barkin' at somethin' down in the creek bed, Joe. Let's git closer." Bushes growin' over the bank hide the creek, so I creep down hopin' for a clear shot that won't hit Tater. Momma whispers, "Be careful," over 'n over like I'm gonna do somethin' crazy. I kneel on the bank 'n lean over lookin' up the creek.

"See anythin'?" Momma asks.

"Somethin's in the water, but it ain't movin'." I put one foot on a rock in the creek bed 'n strain my eyes to make out the hump risin' a little 'bove the water line in the middle o' the creek.

"Hey!" I holler, aimin' the gun. It don't move. "Reckon it's a dead hog or somethin', Momma."

"All right, call Tater off 'n leave it to the buzzards."

I release the hammer on the shotgun. When I start to climb out o' the creek bed, a dark clump catches my eye in the weeds on the other bank.

"Looks like somebody done lost a hat." Momma presses down a bush with the wash pot paddle to look where I point.

"Sho'ly...Holy Jesus," she cries. "That's somebody down in that water!" I scramble to where she stands 'n see what Tater's cornered—a man wearin' Union colors.

"His face is under water, he must be dead," she whines. I run over 'n call Tater off 'is capture.

"Good boy, Tater, you done cornered a bluecoat prisoner." Momma picks up a rock 'n throws it at the body to make sure he ain't playin' possum.

"O Lordy, Lordy, what we gonna do now?" Momma starts her worryin' walk. She paces up 'n down the bank huggin' herself 'n whinin'. "We can't leave 'im here on Massa Carter's land. Capt'n Wirtz'll put us in stocks for hidin' a prisoner."

"But, we ain't hidin' 'im, Momma. He's dead."

"Run back to the house 'n get two shovels. We gotta bury this soldier 'fore he turns up missin'."

"Yessum."

"Take Tater 'n tie 'im up so he won't dig up the grave…'n fetch that ragged sheet off the clothesline. We gotta give this man a proper buryin'.'"

I run fast as I can back to the house thinkin' 'bout haulin' that big Yankee outta the creek. Me 'n Momma need help, but that'll be courtin' more trouble 'n we already got. It took four men to bury one prisoner yesterday. We gotta have a mule. Ben's too little to haul a man's body outta the creek.

After I get the shovels 'n sheet, I tie Tater up on the porch. Then I harness one o' the mules to a plow hitch 'n drive 'im back to the creek. Momma's already turned the body over 'n propped 'is head outta the water on a rock. She looks up 'n sees me with the mule.

"Mercy me, Joe, you done used yo' head."

I loosen the hitch 'n loop the lines 'round the man's shoulders to drag 'im outta the creek.

"He's cavalry, Momma."

"How you know?"

"By the yellow stripe on 'is pants."

"I tol' you not to mess with prisoners in the stockade, Joe."

"Yessum."

She forgot 'bout the paroled bluecoats that work in the camp 'n sometimes buy peanuts from me with real Union tokens. No use in worryin' Momma too much. She holds the dead man's head up while I drive the mule.

"That's far 'nough. Don't wanna go up on the ridge, somebody might see us."

"Ho, mule." I pull off the harness. Diggin' a grave by the creek is fine by me 'cause the ground's softer down here. Momma marks four corners with a shovel, tryin' not to look at the man's face no more'n she has to.

"Want me to see what's in 'is pockets?" I ask.

"Lordy, chile. What's the matter with you? We ain't the kinda people that rob the dead. Leave 'im be."

"I wonder what's 'is name."

"It don't matter now, jist fetch 'is hat."

I use a long dead limb to fish the hat off the bank on the other side o' the creek. The little crossed sabers on the front are muddy, so I clean 'em with my thumb. I see some letters stitched inside the headband, probably his name, but I can't read 'em.

Momma looks at the letters 'n shrugs 'er shoulder. "Uh-huh. Put the hat over 'is face, Joe, 'n start diggin'." I put my foot to the shovel 'n turn over a clod o' black dirt.

"Reckon what killed 'im?"

"Probably slipped on a mossy rock 'n drowned. Don't matter none. Hurry up, we're losin' daylight."

As the sun goes down, we've dug the grave only knee deep. Water starts to seep in, so Momma tells me to climb up 'n help 'er outta the hole. She spreads the sheet on the ground next to the dead cavalryman. We roll 'im over to the middle o' the sheet.

"Momma, there's somethin' stickin' outta his back pocket."

"O Lordy, I reckon it won't hurt nothin' to look," she says. I pull at the corner o' the soggy folded paper, bein' careful not to tear it. Momma unfolds the envelope.

"The writin's faded. Looks like a letter. Wish I could read what it says."

She tucks the letter in 'er apron pocket. Missy Carter showed Momma how to read some, but she plays like she can't. She don't want to get Missy Carter in trouble. I hope she's gonna teach me to read 'n write someday. All the learnin' I know is cipherin' numbers.

We drag the dead man over b'side the long hole in the ground. Momma folds the sides o' the sheet to cover 'is body. We push 'im in the grave 'n water splashes when he hits the bottom. Momma stands over the grave wipin' 'er hands on 'er apron 'n bows 'er head.

"Swing low, sweet chair-ee-oh, come 'n carry the soul o' this poor soldier home. Bless 'is mama 'n papa...'n help this awful war to end soon." Momma lifts up 'er chin 'n looks at the darkenin' sky. She moans', "Lord, set us free 'fore we die."

We fill the grave with dirt 'n mark the corners with rocks.

"Joe, you come back in the mornin' 'n pile rocks over this fresh dirt to keep varmints from diggin' up this po' soldier's body. Then scatter some limbs 'n pine straw over the rocks so it won't look like a grave."

"Yessum."

I belly up on the mule to ride back to the cabin. Momma walks b'hind as night creeps over the field.

"Momma?"

"Uh huh."

"If you figure out that bluecoat's family name, you reckon we could borrow it? He won't be needin' it"

Momma don't answer. She starts to hummin' like she does when she can't think o' nothin' to say. Closer to the cabin, she breaks out singin', "Swing low, sweet charee-o-oh, comin' fo' to carry me home…"

3

Dark falls over us 'fore we get back to the cabin but the moon ain't come up yet. The cows bawl, waitin' to be milked; Ben brays for corn 'n chickens done gone to roost. I slide off the mule in the dark. Momma finds a match in 'er pocket 'n strikes it. Then she takes a lightered stick from under the wash pot 'n makes a torch. The rich pine catches on fast. I fetch the lantern from the porch 'n Momma touches the flame to the wick.

"Come on, I'll hold the light for you to put up the mule."

After unhitchin' the mule I throw some hay in the troughs 'n let the cows in the barn. Momma hangs the lantern 'tween the stalls so we can milk both cows at the same time.

"Does Mr. Dukes need anythin' from the farm?" Momma asks to the tune of little streams of milk squirtin' into the buckets.

"Yessum, he said come tomorrow."

"First thing in the mornin' go pick two or three bushels o' corn 'n dig up some sweet potatoes. Save the peas for us to eat, so leave 'em be."

My mind ain't on pickin' corn or peas or anythin' else, not even milkin'. I keep seein' the cavalryman's cold blue face 'fore I put 'is hat over it. I wonder 'bout 'is ghost. Will it hang 'round 'n haunt our cabin 'fore goin' on to glory? I know I'll be 'wake all night lookin' for signs.

"I don't hear no milk comin' out!"

"Yessum." I start squeezin' the teats 'gain still thinkin' 'bout ghosts. We finish milkin' 'n I pour mine into Momma's bucket. She wedges a wood stopper over the top.

"Tote this milk to the springhouse so it'll stay cool 'til mornin'. Then I'll churn up some butter and buttermilk to trade with Mr. Dukes."

"Yessum."

She holds the lantern on the way to the springhouse. We walk back to the cabin not talkin' much.

"You mighty quiet, Joe, cat got yo' tongue?"

"No'm."

"Then wash up while I fix supper." She leaves me at the well in the dark 'n fetchs me 'nother oil lamp so I can see to draw water. I move the well cover back, push the long bucket in the hole 'n slide my hand over the barrel o' the winch so it won't go down too fast 'n tangle the rope. Drawin' water used to be too hard for me 'til I growed a bit taller. I pour some water in the oak bucket 'n take it to the washstand on the back stoop. Tater follows me whinin' 'til I pour some water in 'is little trough.

All cleaned up, I take the oil lamp inside through the kitchen to the other room 'n set it on the mantle over the fireplace. We got jist two rooms in the cabin, but that's 'nough for me 'n Momma. We eat in one 'n sleep in the other. Everythin' else, we do outside.

"Come eat supper, such as 'tis," Momma calls me to the kitchen. She unwraps a hunk o' cornpone she keeps wrapped in the top of the wood stove, breaks off a piece 'n divides it 'tween us. The cornbread's been warmin' in the stove all day, but crumbled in cool buttermilk it's jist fit to eat. Momma picks at 'er food like she's worried 'bout somethin'. Shoot, I don't let worryin' 'bout a ghost keep me from cleanin' my bowl. After I'm done Momma's got plenty left.

I can't leave the table 'til Momma's through eatin', so I sit real quiet watchin' shadows from the lantern flame dance on the kitchen walls. I play like they're Rebel soldiers followin' Major Carter to war. Then I switch sides 'n play like Yankee soldiers're comin' to turn prisoners loose from the stockade. I don't know which side I'm on. The field hands that ran off said they're gonna hide in the swamp 'til the Yankees come to set us free.

When Massa Carter went to the war he told Momma, *Della, stay here until I come back and we'll talk about your future.* I reckon he's got somethin' in mind for me too.

Momma gits up from the table. "Give Tater my scraps, cause that's all we got to feed 'im."

"Yessum." I take Tater to the front porch 'n scrape 'is supper into the wood bowl I carved from poplar. A faint light over the trees to the East shows the moon's 'bout to rise over Camp Sumter. I hunker down to watch, 'n wonder when the bloodhounds'll come sniffin' out the cavalryman's trail. A dog howls far 'way; I cock my head to make out the breed. Sounds like a possum dog 'stead o' bloodhound; that puts my mind at ease. Momma comes to the porch 'n hangs a dishrag on the rail to dry. The moon peeps through the pine tops.

"Reckon we gonna have a full moon t'night, Momma?"

"Reckon so." She sets the lantern down 'n blows out the flame. "It's the Lord's way o' savin' us po' folk from usin' precious oil." She sets in the cane bottom chair 'n hums a tune that nearly puts me to sleep.

Then Momma stops hummin'. Tater lets out a low growl. A funny feelin' crawls deep inside my bones. Momma feels it too.

"Shush, Tater," she whispers. Momma leaves 'er seat 'n moseys over to the edge o' the porch, lookin' over the cornfield again.

"What's the matter?"

"Shush," she answers. I stand up 'n rub sleep from my eyes to stare over the moonlit corn stalks. After a few minutes o' dead quiet, the wind picks up, rattlin' the magnolia leaves next to the big house.

"Reckon we gonna git some rain soon. Wind's from the west 'n that ol' moon's tryin' to make a ring 'round itself." Momma's talkin' 'bout weather but she ain't thinkin' 'bout rain. Tater growls again, this time a bit louder.

"Momma, do dogs know 'bout ghosts?"

She jerks 'er head 'round 'n cuts them big eyes at me. "Why you askin' 'bout devil stuff, Joe?" I shrug my shoulders kinda 'shamed for rilin' my momma. "Tater knows jist what his nose tells 'im 'n far's I know, haints ain't got no smell." She laughs, but it ain't real. "Time for sleep, Joe, 'fore that full moon gets inside yo' head."

I go in 'n slip off my shoes 'n overalls. Momma's still on the porch with 'er arms folded 'n eyes fixed on the cornfield. I crawl on my pallet 'n wonder what's goin' 'round in 'er mind. She comes inside, closes the door 'n pulls in the latchstring.

"Time to go to the Lord in prayer," she says, kneelin' down b'side my pallet. She prays a long, long prayer like she used to when the war first started. She dwells on askin' the Lord to protect me from evil, sin, sickness, hurt, pain 'n hunger. But she don't ask the Lord to give us a family name, never does. She goes on 'bout lyin' down in green pastures 'n walkin' through the shadow 'o death. Again she says the part 'bout protectin' me like she 'spects somethin' bad's gonna happen 'fore we wake up. I wonder if she figures the corporal's ghost'll come in the middle o' the night? Now, I git worried. "Amen", she says, 'n stands up.

"Momma, can Tater sleep by me tonight?"

"What's the matter, Joe? You scared?"

She's speakin' the truth, but I don't want 'er to think I'm 'fraid o' the cavalryman's ghost wanderin' through the cabin.

"No, Momma, I reckon Tater's growlin' 'cause he's scared."

"Scared o' what?"

"He ain't never seen a dead man 'fore today. I think he's scared to sleep on the porch by hisself." Momma laughs as she unlatches the door 'n calls Tater inside. He curls up 'side me 'n I pull 'im close. Momma blows out the oil lamp 'n 'er bed creaks as she crawls in. The moon's high now; it shines through the window on me 'n Tater as we fall asleep.

~~~

Ol' red rooster crows at first light, roustin' me 'n Momma from our beds. Tater stands by the door, wantin' out. I go out through the kitchen so he can tag 'long with me to the outhouse. 'Stead o' followin' me, Tater takes off 'round the cabin to the cornfield 'n starts barkin'. I finish my b'iness in the outhouse 'n chase after 'im.

"Come on back you crazy dog 'n quit barkin' at that dead Yankee." He goes on point at the edge o' the cornfield. "Back, Tater, ain't no time for huntin' birds." I slap my hands together to make 'im break point 'n come back with me to the cabin. "Good dog, Tater, let's go git some breakfast."

Momma puts some fried fat back 'n gravy on my plate 'n I sop it up with what's left o' the cornbread.

"Don't bother coverin' up that grave right now, Joe. We got more'n we can do 'fore haulin' goods over to the camp." I finish breakfast 'n go feed the livestock. Momma fetches milk from the spring 'n starts churnin'. I git three empty feed sacks from the barn loft 'n set out to pick corn. Tater's worrisome. He tries to slip off to the creek, but I call 'im back more'n a dozen times. He don't know we took care o' that dead Yankee he thought he'd captured.

The sun gits high in the sky 'fore we load the wagon 'n hitch the mules. Momma fries sliced sweet potatoes to eat on our way to Camp Sumter. I tie a rope 'round Tater's neck so he won't run off 'n tangle with the bloodhounds at the camp when we get there. I ain't got time to roast peanuts to sell this trip. A dead Yankee cavalryman kept me busy yesterday. Momma ties a bonnet on 'er head 'n waits for me to help 'er up on the wagon. She looks over our goods; three bushel sacks o' corn, a sack o' sweet potatoes, three bricks o' butter 'n a gallon o' buttermilk.

"Let's hurry on, Joe, 'fore that scorchin' sun melts the butter n' spoils the milk." I drive the mules down the trail 'n turn on the road to the prison.

Halfway to the camp Momma draws the apron up to 'er nose.
"I declare, if that stockade don't stink worse every time we come."
That's what she said the last time 'n the time 'fore that. "The Lord
oughta send a big rain 'n wash that place out good." She gives me
the rest o' the sweet potatoes. "Here, you eat what's left; that
smell done got my appetite."

When we drive by the burial ditches, I stand up to see the
shallow grave I watched them bluecoat prisoners dig yesterday.

"What you lookin' at, Joe?" Momma asks.

"Nothin', Momma, jist stretchin' my legs." The grave's still
there, but why not; it ain't goin' nowhere. "I hate them spooky
woods up there." I set down 'n pop the lines to hurry the mules
down the road.

"You gotta quit listenin' to that crazy corporal tryin' to scare
you silly. I oughta take the cur by the ear an' give 'im a piece o'
my mind." I know Momma's not serious, 'cause she can't talk
back to a white man without gettin' whupped. I bite my lip 'n
push the team through the patch o' woods to Stockade Creek.
After we cross that stink-water stream to the camp, a few reserves
hurry to meet the wagon when they see us comin'.

"You got any molasses or onions today?" a guard hollers 'n
waves paper money in 'is hand.

Momma shakes 'er head, "Keep on goin'. We gotta make it
to the store 'fore them boys take our goods off the wagon."
Momma knows the hungry guards'll pay, but Mr. Dukes gits mad
if we peddle to them first. He's the boss o' vittles in the camp. I
pop the mules to make 'em run fast to the store. The reserves cuss
'n drop back. Mr. Dukes hears our racket 'n comes out to the
porch with two reserves carryin' rifles.

"Howdy Della, howdy Joe, it's hotter'n the devil's wash pot
today."

"Yessuh," Momma says.

"What y'all got good for me today?"

Momma waves 'er hand over the wagon bed singin' out what
we brought, "We got some nice new dug yams, sweet corn, butter

'n buttermilk, fresh churned this mornin'." The guards lick their
lips like they tastin' it right now.

"Lemme see what I'll give for the lot," Red Dukes says
pokin' 'is fat fingers at the sacks. Momma shakes 'er head 'fore he
even makes a' offer. "A pound o' chicory, er...make that two
pounds; a half sack o' flour; a pound o' sugar and two pounds o'
salt." Then he turns 'round like he's goin' inside to fetch 'is trade
goods.

Momma pulls on the sack under 'er seat. "I reckon you don't
want none o' my butter 'n buttermilk."

Mr. Dukes turns 'round 'n drops his jaw like he don't b'lieve
what he hears. "Now, of course I do, Della. I counted that in the
trade."

Momma pokes out 'er lips 'n shakes 'er head faster. "Mr.
Dukes suh, you know I don't use no chicory. I gotta have a whole
sack o' flour, some meal—the good kind with no ground up
cobs—more'n a pound o' sugar. I got plenty 'o salt, but I can use
some fat back 'n molasses." Mr. Dukes scratches 'is head 'n po'
mouths 'bout how hard goods are to come by. Momma squints 'er
eyes while he carries on. "Mr. Dukes, you know when Massa
Carter comes back, the first thing he's gonna ask is, 'Della, did you
make fair trades on goods from the farm?' I gave 'im my word to
give account."

Mr. Dukes spreads 'is hands 'n acts innocent. I reckon he
likes to make Momma think she out-trades him, but he sometimes
slips in a tin o' snuff 'n a stick o' molasses candy with the goods.
The two guards unload our wagon as Mr. Dukes fetches 'is trade
goods from the store.

He drops the last sack in the wagon. "My men'll see y'all
out of the camp so the bluecoat parolees won't steal your
supplies." The guards follow our wagon to the creek 'n then turn
back.

"It ain't the bluecoats that worry me," Momma says as we
head to the woods. "It's them reserves; they look like they ain't
had 'nough to eat to keep a dog alive. The devil takes hold o'

hungry men's souls 'n wrings out all the goodness; us good folk jist git in their way."

I slap the reins 'gainst the mules' rumps to git 'long through the woods. I slack off the lines to slow up the mules when we're past the death ditches. That lonesome grave by the underbrush pulls my eyes to it 'n won't let go. Why ain't the buzzards circlin' overhead? It's been a whole day since the bluecoat prisoners left 'em a carcass for the takin'. Maybe the dead man ain't got 'nough meat on 'is bones to feed the buzzards a proper dinner.

4

We unload the goods from Mr. Dukes' store 'fore I unhitch the mule team. Tater jumps out o' the wagon 'n takes off through the cornfield.

"Tater, come back to me boy!" Like a lightenin' bolt, he's gone to find the cavalryman we buried.

Momma pays Tater no mind. She's gettin' ready to wash off the dust, lice 'n fleas from the camp.

"Help me with the washtub," Momma hollers from the back yard. I run to the wash bench 'n help 'er tote the big wood tub to the back porch. Momma hands me a yella cake o' lye soap. "You go on down 'n bathe in the creek while I wash off."

"But Momma…"

"Don't go buttin' yo' momma like a billy goat; now go on so I can git in the tub."

"Momma, do I hafta go to the creek?"

Momma straightens up 'n pokes out 'er lips. "Umm huh, you done let that dead Yankee mess up yo' mind." Momma closes 'er eyes 'n cocks 'er head like she's studyin' my worry.

"Go draw me some water for the kettle, Joe." I hop off the stoop, go over to the well 'n lower the bucket. Momma watches me crank the winch. "What'd you do with the soap, Joe?"

"It's on the stoop."

"All right, you fetch that soap 'n go on down to the creek. Find Tater 'n y'all go upstream, way past where he found the dead man. Make 'im stay with you while you wash so nothin'll bother you."

I still don't wanna go to the creek, but Momma's set 'er mind this time. I pour water in the oak bucket 'n haul it to the stoop. Momma takes a jar off the shelf 'n dips out some sticky stuff like molasses that smells like pine tar 'n sulfur. She dabs it in my hair.

"This potion'll kill the varmints in yo' hair." I don't know if this stinky stuff works, but now I gotta wash my hair for sure.

Kickin' off my shoes, I run barefoot through the cornfield 'n down towards the creek. Tater comes up over the ridge 'n wags 'is tail when he hears my whistle. He barks like he wants me to follow 'n turns up the creek 'way from the place we buried the cavalryman.

"Hold back, Tater, we ain't chasin' rabbits right now." He roams 'round the pine thicket while I look for a bathin' hole in the creek. The water's so low it takes a while to find a knee-deep pool with a sandy bottom. I hang my clothes on a gum saplin' 'n wade to the middle. First thing I gotta do is wash the sulfur smell outta my hair. If lice 'n fleas have noses, one sniff o' this stuff'll keel 'em over dead for sure.

Tater ain't doin' 'is job watchin' over me, so I whistle 'n holler.

"Come on, Tater, I'm 'bout done." He strikes a trail up stream, lets out a yelp 'n takes off half barkin' 'n half howlin' like he's chasin' a rabbit. Pretty soon, Tater gives up 'n comes back to the creek draggin' 'is tongue in front 'n his tail behind. He sprawls 'is front paws in the creek 'n laps at the water.

"It's too hot for runnin' rabbits, Tater-dog, way too hot." He comes over for a pat on the head, but backs away. He don't like the smell o' sulfur any more'n I do.

Suddenly, Tater stiffens like he's 'bout to go on point. "What is it, Tater?" He growls 'n moves real slow towards the bank. "Good boy, good boy, take it easy."

Standin' tall to look, I don't see nothin', don't heah nothin', but my skin crawls like somethin's stalkin' me. I ease over to get my clothes, might have to run from a bear. Tater goes to the other bank, still growlin' 'n movin' one step at a time toward a big stand o' blackberry vines thicker'n hedge bushes. I figure he ain't barkin' 'cause it might be a polecat hidin' in the thicket. He's messed with a polecat b'fore 'n he's had 'nough o' that.

"Come on back, Tater, heah boy!" Tater quits growlin' but 'stead o' comin' to me he strikes a point. Now, Tater ain't no bird dog, but sometimes he'll point bobwhites or doves. He won't break point 'til I go 'n flush the birds out o' the blackberry vines.

"Hold 'em boy, I'm comin'." I pick up a stick 'n wade 'cross the creek. Tater stands still while I creep closer. "Good boy, I'll flush 'em out so we can go back to the cabin." Ripe blackberries cover the bush; so many I wish I'd brought a bucket to pick 'em. I push the stick under the bush so I won't knock any berries off. Nothin' flies out.

"Scat birds, scat outta there." Still, nothin' moves.

I'm sure there's a bird or two in the vines 'cause my dog's nose don't lie. I don't wanna get any closer with my bare feet, so I circle 'round the blackberry vines tryin' to see Tater's birds. On the other side I shake the stick under the vines again 'n then stop to listen.

Nothin'.

The woods're quiet as death. Not a sound anywhere, no crows fussin', no doves callin', not even wind whistlin' through the pine trees. My skin crawls again. I get a whiff o' somethin' mighty familiar, like burnt pine, sweat, 'n Stockade Creek. Can't be the stockade 'cause the smell never comes this far from camp.

Somethin' moves b'hind me. A big hand slaps over my mouth 'n a strong arm presses my chest, holdin' me still.

"Be quiet, boy. I won't hurt you." A man's rough whiskers scratch my ear. He whispers, "Just relax." I can't see 'is face, but I catch 'is blue pants out o' the corner o' my eye. It's a Yankee bluecoat from the stockade. He's gonna kill me!

"You're the peanut boy, aren't you?" I try to nod my head. "Promise you won't shout and I'll uncover your mouth." I nod again. "Tell me your name." He takes 'is hand off my mouth. I gasp for fresh air.

I mouth my name, but nothin' comes out.

"Easy now, there's no cause to fear me. I have a boy about your age back home. You believe me?"

He loosens 'is hold on my chest but won't let go my wrist. His face is smutty, with dark red spots all over. I look into 'is gray eyes for signs o' truth. He talks kind, a lot like Massa Carter, 'cept he's s'posed to be a killer bluecoat.

"Well, do you?" I take a deep breath 'n nod my head. "Good, now call your dog."

My mouth's too dry to whistle so I try to holler, "Heah, Tater."

"Again, he didn't hear you."

I call louder. I really want Tater to turn tail 'n go git Momma. But he comes 'round the blackberry vines waggin' 'is tail 'stead o' barkin' 'n growlin' like he did at the dead cavalryman. Maybe he can't see the man holdin' me. Maybe it's the cavalryman's ghost got hold o' me. Tater comes right up 'n sniffs the man's leg like he's family.

"Don't worry, son, the dog is *niji*. He led you to me."

I don't know why this strange man calls my dog that name. "His name's Tater."

"So I hear when you call him. He is also *niji*."

I try to pull 'way from the man, but he holds my wrist tighter. "But you're a bluecoat. Capt'n Wirtz 'll hang me, 'n my momma too. Lemme go!" I start to cry. "He'll send Turner's bloodhounds after you."

The man turns me loose. I want to run away, but my feet won't move. He sets down cross-legged on the pine straw 'n scratches Tater 'hind the ears.

"Don't worry, son, the bloodhounds won't come," he says with a calm voice that settles me down. I crumble to the ground 'n cross my legs the same as his.

"How...how do you know?"

"Because I'm dead."

I knew it! He's a ghost!

"The captain sent a crew to bury me yesterday."

"D-d-d-dead?"

"Officially dead, but you can see I have not entered the spirit world yet. I can't tell you more, but I need your help."

"I can't do nothin' for you Mister. My momma's waitin' for me to come back 'n help with the chores." I ain't so sure I trust this 'scaped prisoner who thinks he's dead, or 'bout dead.

He rubs sweat from 'is eyes with 'is dirty sleeve that used to be white. Some o' the red spots come off on 'is sleeve, but he ain't bleedin'!

"I know you can't stay here, but I need just two things from you." He leans towards me like he's gonna tell a secret. "I want you to promise on your honor that you won't tell anybody about seeing me, at least for a few days. Can I have your word on that?"

I can't make a promise like that 'less I aim to keep it. If I tell, I'll go back to prison with this bluecoat.

"I hafta tell Momma. We don't have no secrets."

"Do you want to put her in harm's way? Like you said, if Captain Wirtz finds out, he'll arrest her as a traitor. And your father won't be able to save her."

"I ain't got no daddy."

"Oh, I didn't know. Was he in Lee's army?"

"I never had no daddy." The bluecoat rubs 'is head like he's confused or maybe he's tired o' me gettin' on 'is nerves.

"I can't let you go unless you pledge to hold your tongue." The man reaches out 'n grabs my wrist real tight. I don't wanna give in, but I nod my head, 'fraid he's gonna hurt me. "You have to say it, son, say it out loud."

"Yessuh."

"I mean the whole promise."

"Yessuh, I promise not to tell Momma."

"Or anybody else?"

"Ain't nobody else to tell, just me 'n Momma."

He turns me loose 'n reaches into 'is blue pants pocket. They ain't got no yellow stripe like the dead cavalryman's, jist plain. He puts out 'is hand 'n shows me a little clump o' brown leaves all wadded up. He pinches off half the wad 'n hands it to me.

"Here, take this *kinikinic*. It's a sign of my thanks for your pledge of secrecy."

He puts the dried leaves in my hand. My eyes jump back 'n forth from my hand to 'is eyes. He closes 'is hand 'n puts it to 'is nose, takin' a deep breath like he's drawin' in some kind o' power from the leaves. I pull my hand up to my nose 'n sniff slowly.

"Smells like tobacco."

"Yes, it's *assema*, tobacco, mixed with willow bark and called *kinikinic*." Then he wraps 'is other hand 'round mine 'n smiles for the first time since he sneaked up on me. "*Kinikinic* binds us together. We are *niji*."

I shake my head. "But that's what you called Tater?"

"*Niji* means brother, friend. You and I are now like family. And Tater too."

This man from Yankee land talks different. His words are pointy but flow smooth like creek water over rocks. I don't understand, but nod like I do.

"You said you need two things; what else?"

The man stands up 'n tells me to put the tobacco in my pocket. He does the same.

"I haven't had a bath in clean branch water since before I was captured at the Wilderness. I wonder if you would let me use your soap. I'd be mighty grateful."

I forgot 'bout the soap. I lead him to my washin' hole 'n point to the soap.

"Go on home, brother, and remember..." He puts 'is finger on my lips. "Silence. Come back tomorrow, I need some food."

I nod 'n start up the rise towards the cabin, but Tater stays with the man. I whistle twice 'fore that stubborn dog comes.

"Tater, you're one mess o' watchdog," I squeeze 'is ear. "You didn't bark 'n carry on at that bluecoat like you did at the dead cavalryman. How'd you know he wouldn't hurt me? What kind o' spell did that bluecoat put on you? I wish you could talk."

Walkin' slow's a terrapin through the cornfield gives me time to figure out what to tell Momma. Maybe she won't ask no questions. Trouble waits for me at the cabin 'cause I can't tell 'er no lies. But how can I keep the promise to my *niji*?

5

I head straight for the barn so Momma won't see me 'n ask a lot o' questions. The best place to go is up the ladder to the loft where my peanut crop's dryin'. I pick out a dozen bunches 'n drop 'em through the ladder hole to roast in the wash pot. I hear Momma talkin' to somebody so I stop to listen. A man answers 'er. It sounds like Massa Carter. He's come back from the war!

I run to the front o' the house where Massa Carter's carriage with 'is big bay mare stands at the hitchin' post. On the other side, a freight wagon's backed up to the porch. My stomach flips over. The war must be over 'n Massa Carter's come home! Missy Carter's done brought 'er stuff back from Macon. But then I see Momma's walkin' in circles huggin' 'er ribs like somethin's wrong. My stomach flips over again.

A man comes out with a bunch o' sheets in 'is arms 'n Momma follows 'im to the wagon. Somethin' bad must 'o happened 'cause I don't see Massa Carter. The man stacks the sheets in the wagon while 'nother man brings 'im some more. The men go back inside.

Momma rubs 'er hands over the pile o' sheets. "Lordy, them men don't know how to handle fine linen," she grumbles under her breath. Her face shinin' with tears, she stacks the sheets in a neat pile.

I slip up behind Momma 'n put my hand on 'er back.

"Momma?" She jumps back like she don't know it's me.

"Lordy, Joe, don't sneak up on me like that!" She wipes the tears with 'er apron.

"What's wrong, Momma?"

"O Lordy, Massa Carter's done got hisself hurt in the war. He's in a hospital 'n might be dyin'.'" She starts to bawl again. "Po' Missy Carter, she don't know what to do." I don't know if Momma's cryin' over Missy Carter or Massa Carter.

Missy Carter's daddy, Mr. Jim, comes down the steps with more blankets. "Howdy, Joe, where you been, cavorting with the Yankees?" My heart stops! He's found out 'bout the bluecoat prisoner we buried. Then he laughs 'n hands the bundle to Momma. His eyes roam up 'n down me like seein' me for the first time. "And I see you've grown a bit taller."

"Yessuh."

The other two men bring out 'nother load. Mr. Jim turns back to the b'iness at hand. "Is that all?"

"Except for some tablecloths in the dining room closet. Do we take those too?"

Momma straightens up 'n hollers, "Lordy, no, don't take Missy Carter's fancy cloths. They don't make good bandages no how." Mr. Jim coughs. Momma tucks 'er head real quick 'n stares at the wagon wheel avoidin' Mr. Jim's squintin' eyes 'n tight lips.

"Mind your tongue, Della, you haven't been freed yet!" Mr. Jim growls. "Yeah, bring 'em on boys, my daughter can decide which stuff to send to the hospital."

The men finish packin' the wagon 'n head the mule team down the trail slow 'nuff fo' Mr. Jim to catch up. "Where're they takin' Missy Carter's goods, Momma?"

"Hush up, chile, I gotta help close up the house." She follows Mr. Jim into the house with me taggin' 'long. They go 'round closin' the window curtains 'gain to shut out the light. Dust flies everywhere 'n makes me sneeze.

"Git outta the house an' wait for me, Joe!"

"Yessum." It ain't a good time to talk back, so I go outside. Tater sets on the porch keepin' watch over Massa Carter's bay mare. They used to be good buddies 'fore Missy Carter moved that beauty to Macon. The mare snorts, talkin' to me. I reach out to rub the white blaze runnin' down 'er nose.

"Hey Lasses, good girl." She got that name bein' the color o' molasses. I long to ride 'er again now that I'm big 'nough to set in the saddle by myself 'stead o' ridin' double with Massa Carter.

The front door slams shut behind me. Mr. Jim clicks the lock 'n tells Momma, "Don't go spreading the word about Major Carter's injury. Those reserves at the camp might get the idea he won't be coming back to this place. They'll start circling like buzzards waiting for a chance to move in and rustle y'all out."

"Yessuh," she says. Mr. Jim jerks 'is head 'round like he's been shot. Momma changes 'er tune. "I mean, nawsuh, I won't tell a soul."

"That's what I thought you meant." Mr. Jim unties Lasses' reins 'n climbs into the carriage. "Hey Joe, I'm real short of hands. How about coming with me to help out?"

I duck my head pretendin' I don't hear. Momma says, "Massa Jim, my boy's the only help I got mindin' this place. Please don't take 'im 'way from me."

"Hmmph, don't see enough crops on this place to shake a stick at. I'll talk to the Major about what to do with Joe," he says. He taps the mare's rump with the reins. "Giddy-up, hoss, let's go."

Momma folds 'er arms 'n starts the worryin' walk. "Hard times a comin', this war ain't done with us yet."

"Do I hafta go to Macon?" I'm catchin' Momma's worry fever. She jist keeps on walkin' back towards the cabin payin' me no mind.

"Momma?"

She stops 'n puts 'er hands on my shoulders. "We gonna take one day at a time like the Lord says. Right now, I got 'nough on my mind to sprout horns. Massa Carter's done got struck down 'n Missy Carter's goin' to 'is side." Momma's eyes fill with tears again.

"Why she doin' that?"

"'Cause gen'ral somebody done sent a letter sayin' Massa Carter's in a hospital 'n they got no mo' bandages. He tol' Missy Carter to gather up all 'er sheets 'n blankets 'n bring 'em to the hospital. That's all he wrote. Them Confederates should o' had 'nough sense to stock up on bandages 'fore they went 'n started a war. Men hankerin' for a fight don't think 'bout the next day."

My head starts buzzin' 'bout goin' up to Macon 'n leavin' Momma, but she don't need no mo' worries in her pile right now. The day ain't done yet. There's plenty 'o time to start peanuts roastin' 'fore supper. I go set the iron wash pot right side up 'n brush the dirt off the rim. After settin' the pot legs on flat rocks, I pile hardwood sticks under it, ready to fire up.

I run to the kitchen, open the stove 'n poke a lightered stick in the coals. I'm waitin' for the kindlin' to catch on 'n Momma asks me a question I don't wanna hear.

"I can't find the soap, Joe, where'd you put it?"

Gotta have time to think. "Let me go start my fire 'n I'll look for it." I take my stick o' fire to the wash pot fast as I can without the flame blowin' out. The fire starts up good, so I fetch the peanuts from the barn. I shake the dried dirt off the clumps wonderin' what to tell Momma 'bout the soap. There're two things she won't put up with—lyin' 'n wastin' good soap. Gotta go find what's left o' that lye soap the bluecoat took.

It takes two turns to fetch the peanuts from the barn. I kneel on the ground 'n take my time pullin' 'em off the vines 'n flippin' 'em in the wash pot. Massa Carter showed me how to roast peanuts. He said: *Taste one raw peanut from each clump first, to make sure they're fit to eat. Shake off every speck of dirt before you throw 'em in the pot. Just cover the bottom and then add one more layer. Let the wood burn down until the flames turn the coals red-hot. Rake the coals around the pot and let 'em cook a little more than one hour. Stir the peanuts around with a stick and leave 'em cooking until the coals turn black. Then they'll be done and fit to eat.*

I used to set on the front porch with Massa Carter eatin' roasted peanuts 'n throwin' empty shells under the hedges. He said they make good fertilizer, but Missy Carter fussed 'cause we made a mess.

I rake hot coals 'round the wash pot 'n head for the barn to feed the livestock. Momma hollers from the cabin porch. "Joe, come 'ere quick!"

Uh oh, she ain't forgot 'bout the missin' soap. When I look up, I know somethin's wrong, but it ain't the lye soap on 'er mind. She's huggin' 'erself 'n lookin' towards the big house. She comes down the steps with Tater at 'er heels 'n meets me in the yard.

"Stand still 'n listen, Joe." I do like she says, but I don't hear nothin'. Tater whines 'n cocks one ear. "Somebody's comin' down the road. I can't hear 'em but Tater can."

"Maybe Mr. Jim forgot somethin'," I whisper. Tater whimpers 'n backs up 'tween my legs.

"Shh...ush, Tater's tellin' us the bloodhounds're comin'."

"What we gonna do now?"

"Maybe they gonna pass on down the road. Mr. Turner knows we don't..." She stops stone still. "Lordy, Joe, they comin' after that dead man." Momma spins 'round like a top. She starts hollerin' orders like a reserve sergeant. "Joe, get some rope 'n tie Tater to the porch rail. Go tend yo' peanuts like nothin's wrong. I'm gonna hide the shotgun under the mattress 'n set on the porch patchin' yo' overalls. Let me do the talkin' Joe, no matter what happens. If Mr. Turner asks you questions, just hunch yo' shoulders 'n act like you dumb. Do you heah me good?"

"Yessum."

Soon's Momma settles in 'er chair on the porch, I hear bloodhounds bellerin' in the distance. They carry on back 'n forth 'tween deep barkin' 'n howlin', more like they jist sniffin' 'round than follerin' a trail. Soon two rangy bloodhounds come 'round the corner o' the big house strainin' on their leashes. Mr. Turner, Capt'n Wirtz's hired tracker, follers 'em with two rifle-totin' reserves close b'hind—one old man 'n Corporal Jake Tolliver, the meanest guard in the camp. The gun draws out his meanness.

"Howdy Della," Mr. Turner hollers over the barkin' dogs. Tater strains at the rope to protect Momma. Momma jist nods 'n goes right on sewin', not missin' a stitch. "Word's out you had visitors today." My breathin' stops. Momma jist nods. "We're missin' a prisoner from the stockade; figured he'd find his way over here." Momma shakes 'er head, but keeps 'er mouth shut.

Corporal Tolliver moves closer to me 'n sniffs the air like a hound. "Parchin' goobers, huh boy?" I shrug my shoulders like Momma said. "Don't reckon you seen our prisoner did ya?" I shrug my shoulders 'gain. He pulls the rifle off 'is shoulder 'n pokes it in my belly. That sets Momma off. She stomps off the porch right up to Mr. Turner.

"Mr. Turner, suh, what you want from us?"

Mr. Turner barks orders, "Stand down, Corporal. Don't mess with Major Carter's boy." Then he turns to Momma. "One of your visitors was drivin' Major Carter's carriage. Any word from the Major?"

Momma shrugs 'er shoulders, "Mr. Jim come down from Macon on bi'ness for Missy Carter."

"I see, so she's fixin' to move back, is she?"

"I reckon," Momma says.

Mr. Turner huffs a bit like he done got all the information Momma's gonna give out. "Well then, we're just gonna have a look around and see if the dogs can pick up the trail of that prisoner."

"Oh, that's fine with me, suh, if you got nothin' better to do with yo' time."

"All right, men, y'all look in the barn. Me and the dogs'll take a turn around the house and corn crib." Momma stands in the yard while the search goes on. I tend my roastin' peanuts, Tater howls from the porch, 'n Ben brays at the guards in the barn.

Mr. Turner leads the hounds back to the yard as the guards come out o' the barn scatterin' chickens that go sqawkin' 'cross the yard. "Find anything?" Mr. Turner hollers.

"Nothin' but these," Corporal Tolliver shows a hatful o' eggs. "We gonna eat good tonight."

"Corporal! Put those back where you got 'em. We don't take stuff from Major Carter's place." Mr. Turner turns red in the face. Tolliver shakes 'is head. "Put 'em back, I say!"

Tolliver stomps 'is foot 'n screws up 'is face. "You don't know how hungry I am, Turner. B'sides, you don't give me no orders."

Mr. Turner takes a bullwhip off 'is belt 'n pops it in the air. The hounds yelp. Tolliver raises 'is gun with 'is free hand. Momma walks 'tween the feudin' men, right up to the corporal. I hold my breath. She takes two eggs from 'is hat 'n hands 'em to the other guard. Then she takes out two more.

"Suh, I hate to see a soldier starve to death, so I'll hold yo' eggs while you put t'others back."

Time stands still. Momma don't know Tolliver like I do. He's mean 'nough to shoot 'er over a hatful o' eggs. The other guard says, "I'll hold yo' gun." Mister Turner calms the bloodhounds.

Tolliver shifts 'is eyes from Momma to Mr. Turner 'n back many times 'fore handin' 'is gun to the other guard 'n takin' a step towards the barn. Ahhh...I can breathe 'gain. But, 'stead o' puttin' the eggs back in the barn, Tolliver dumps 'em on the ground. He slaps 'is hat back on 'is head, grabs the two eggs from Momma's hands 'n stalks off huffin'.

Shakin' 'is head, Mr. Turner stands on the hounds' leashes so he can roll up 'is bullwhip. "Well, I reckon there're no prisoners around here."

"Nawsuh, Mr. Turner." Just as Momma speaks, one o' the bloodhounds rears up 'n breaks away. It heads straight for me, sniffs at my leg 'n lets out a yelp like a coon dog strikin' a trail.

"What do we have here?" Mr. Turner asks, comin' over to get 'is dog. "Boy, you been cavortin' with bluecoats?" I stand stiff as a hickory board. "What about it, Della, does your boy look like an escaped prisoner. You know my dog's nose never lies." Then he laughs 'n pulls his dog back. "Ought to wash your overalls after coming over to the camp, boy, no telling what you pick up around there."

Momma says, "Yessuh, I'll do jist that." Mr. Turner makes 'is way down the trail talkin' to the bloodhounds. Momma unties Tater so he can lick up the broken eggs. "Go in the house 'n shed yo' clothes, Joe, so I can wash off that cavalryman we buried."

"Yessum." I stir the peanuts 'n go inside to change clothes. Momma don't know she's gonna wash off the smell o' two Yankee prisoners.

6

'Fore ol' red rooster crows I git up to scoop the peanuts outta the wash pot so Momma can do the washin'. And I gotta fetch the soap from the creek 'fore doin' the chores. Momma don't fuss at me 'bout the soap, jist screws up 'er face. It's best to git outta sight this mornin'.

I stash a croaker sack full o' roasted peanuts on the cart to peddle, 'n stuff some in my pockets to trade for the blackberries the bluecoat promised me. I fetch a syrup can from the back stoop to put 'em in.

"Goin' to the creek, be back direc'ly," I holler over my shoulder 'n run 'fore Momma can stop me.

Tater races on by me through the cornfield to help me find *niji*. A thin mornin' fog 'bout knee high settles over the creek.

"*Niji, niji,*" I holler through the fog. Whistlin' wings o' doves takin' off send flutters down my back. The bluecoat don't call back, so I ease on down to the creek 'n find a rocky place to cross over. Tater splashes through the water 'n stops on the other bank.

"Go find *niji.*" He takes off up the rise, 'way from me. I squint tryin' to see through the shadows in the pine thicket. Nothin' moves. I whistle for Tater but he takes off, "You sorry dog, don't you run off." I climb the rise to where Tater went into the woods. He can't track the bluecoat in there. Them scrub bushes're too thick for a man to walk through. I holler one mo' time. Not hearin' him or Tater, I turn 'round to look in the blackberry patch where my *niji* grabbed me from b'hind. I can't b'lieve I'm seein' Tater on point jist like b'fore. This time he points 'way from the blackberry vines 'n up the rise towards me. That crazy dog slipped 'round b'hind me somehow.

"Good boy, Tater, steady...steady. Why you pointin' to that thick pine straw?" I jerk my head 'round to see if *niji*'s sneakin' up on me 'gain. "It's me, *niji*, where you at? Ain't nobody with me...'cept Tater."

Tater holds point 'n I listen for signs of the *niji* I can't see.

"Joe," a faint voice calls, like it's comin' from under a quilt.

"Yessuh." The pine straw at the tip o' Tater's nose wiggles 'n rises off the ground in one big clump. A hand reaches out. The bluecoat pushes back the cover o' pine straw 'n sets up like he's risin' from the dead.

"*Niji?*" I whisper, jist to be sure.

"Joe," he says as he rolls outta the hole, "I'm glad you came back." He stands up 'n brushes trash off 'is shirt 'n pants. "I had to make certain you came alone; didn't mean to scare you."

"Yessuh."

"You don't have to call me sir. I'm only a private. And people call me Frank, not *niji*." I shake my head. He smiles, "*Niji*'s not a name. In the language of my people it's the same as saying 'my friend'."

"Yankee people?"

"Not exactly, Ojibwe people. Did you bring me any food?" I stare at 'im tryin' to figure out what kind o' people he's talkin' 'bout. "Joe, did you hear me?"

"Oh, I got some peanuts." I put the can on the ground 'n empty my pockets into 'is hands. He puts one in his mouth 'n chomps down. "No, wait. They ain't shelled yet." I squeeze a peanut 'tween my thumb 'n fingers, crack it open 'n dump the goody in 'is hand. He chews slow 'n raises 'is eyebrows.

"Huh, tastes a bit like *manomin*."

"*Manomin?*"

"It's food that grows on water back home. Some call it wild rice." He shells the peanuts 'n eats faster'n a pig cleans a trough. I look 'round for the blackberries he promised me. He reads my mind. "I picked some berries, but I was too hungry to save them for you. Come with me, I have something better."

Mr. Frank leads me up the creek through a gum stand to a clearin'. Tater barks 'n scratches 'is paws on a saplin'. There's a rabbit hangin' in the air by its hind legs.

"Poor little critter sprung the trap just before you came. Do you and your mother eat rabbit?"

"We do, suh! Uh…I mean, we do Mr. Frank. Next to fatback, it's Momma's best eatin'." Why's he offerin' me the rabbit? "Don't you wanna eat it, Mr. Frank? We got plenty t'eat."

He laughs. "I had all the raw meat I could stomach in the stockade. If I cook it here, the smoke will draw guards over here like deer flies." He bends the saplin' over 'n takes the rabbit loose. Then he reaches into his back pocket 'n pulls out a piece o' tin wrapped in a cloth. "Don't watch if the sight of blood turns your stomach," he warns me.

"No, no wait," I holler. "Don't kill 'im now. Momma knows I won't bring home a dressed rabbit on a hot day. It won't be fittin' to eat." Mr. Frank cocks 'is head 'n squints 'is eyes at me.

"All right, Joe. I see you have a good deal to teach me about getting along in this Georgia heat." He rips a strip off the cloth wrappin' 'n ties the rabbit's legs together. "You replace this tie before your mother sees it, or she'll wonder where you got a piece of Union army shirt."

"Yessuh…I mean yes, Mr. Frank. I got some string in the barn."

"One other thing, my *niji,* you must thank the rabbit for the gift of life he gave for you. Put a pinch of tobacco on the ground where his blood will flow. Can you do that?" Mr. Frank hands me the rabbit 'n puts his arm 'round my shoulder. I jump back as he touches me. "What's wrong, Joe?" he snaps.

"Er...I reckon you'd best not touch me," I say. The thought o' Mr. Turner's bloodhounds sniffin' at my legs yesterday spooked me good.

"Are you afraid of me?"

"No, Mr. Frank."

"Is it because I'm Indian?"

"Injun?" I study 'is face again, this time lookin' for red skin. It ain't red, but it's darker'n mine.

"Yes, I'm Ojibwe, some call us Chippewa. Why do you shy away from me?"

"It's the bloodhounds."

"Where?" He stands straight 'n turns his head sideways. "I don't hear anything."

"Not today, day b'fore. Mr. Turner brought 'is hounds by the cabin lookin' for that 'scaped cavalryman. And one of 'em..."

"Wait a minute, what cavalryman?" I done let my tongue slip. I clamp my hand over my mouth to keep the rest o' the secret in. But the injun's eyes cut right through me. "Tell me, Joe. Did you see an escaped prisoner around here?"

"I ain't s'posed to say, Momma made me promise." He kneels down in front o' me 'n draws a deep breath. He covers 'is eyes with 'is hands for a minute. Then he pulls 'em down over 'is nose, mouth 'n chin like he's wipin' worry off his face.

"Sit," he says. I ease down on the pine straw holdin' Tater's neck with one hand 'n the rabbit with the other. "A year ago, I left my wife and six children to fight this war to set Negro slaves free. The last thing my boys and girls promised was to obey their mother and to do nothing that might dishonor their father's name. My eldest is almost your age, Joe. I pray that she has your strength to stand by her promises. But, I also pray that she has the wisdom to question those promises when a hungry wolf circles their lodge. Do you understand what that means, Joe?"

"I ain't sure I do."

"If another escaped prisoner has come this way, the bloodhounds could track him down and find me too. And you know that capturing me on your property would be bad for you and your mother. I have to know which way the cavalryman went so I can go a different direction. Now, you don't need to tell me anything, just point. Did he go north?" He points upstream. I shake my head no.

"East?" I shake my head 'gain as he points towards the stockade.

"South?" I shake my head as he points to the woods.

"West?" I shake my head as he runs out o' d'rections to point.

I stand up 'n look all 'round, wonderin' what to do. Without a word, I point to the ground.

"He dug a tunnel?" Mr. Frank asks. I shake my head no.

"He's hidin' in a hole, a cave?" I shake my head again. Mr. Frank scratches 'is head.

I walk back towards the creek with Mr. Frank 'n Tater right b'hind. I pick the soap up off a rock 'n cross to the other side. Tater runs off towards the cavalryman's grave 'n he stops at the pile o' loose dirt, barkin'. I stand by the grave 'n point.

Mr. Frank bends down to rub 'is hand 'cross the dirt. Then he cocks 'is head toward me like I ain't got good sense.

"He's dead?"

I nod.

"What killed him, a guard?"

I shake my head, holdin' on tight to my promise to Momma. Mr. Frank knew I couldn't talk, so he tried 'nother way to find out what happened.

"Show me where you found him." I climb down the creek bank 'n point to the water.

Mr. Frank picks up a pine limb 'n brushes over the trail we made when we dragged the dead man 'cross the sand 'n up the bank. He don't say nothin' but I feel dumb as a fence rail for not thinkin' to cover the tracks.

"Was he shot?" I shake my head, 'cause me 'n Momma didn't see no bullet holes in the man's clothes.

"Did he drown?" Recallin' a bruise on 'is brow, I rub a finger 'tween my eyes to show where the man was hurt.

"He must have slipped and hit his head on a rock; probably drowned. What a shame his freedom didn't last very long." Mr. Frank shakes 'is head 'n climbs up the bank to the grave.

"How did you know he was cavalry?" I cross my fingers on my forehead. Then I slide one finger down the side o' my leg. Still, I don't say nothin' to break my promise.

"Oh, I see, crossed sabers and yellow stripes. He must be one of the men from First Cavalry that dug a tunnel under the fence." Then a sad look makes Mr. Frank's face pale like a ghost. He stands b'side the grave 'n raises 'is hands in the air.

"O *Gitchi Manito,* send this great warrior to the spirit world." Then he takes a pinch o' tobacco from 'is pocket 'n scatters it over the grave. *"Eagle-With-Three-Tongues* bids you *meegwitch* until we meet again in the world of our ancestors."

This strange injun talk makes my feet itch to git movin' outta here. "I gotta go back to the cabin."

"Of course you do, Joe. I need some time to figure out which direction to take from here. Could you bring me a grubstake and some different clothes before I go?"

"I don't know, Mr. Frank. I gotta hurry over to Camp Sumter to peddle peanuts today. Maybe tonight I can slip you a shirt 'n pants from Massa Carter's house, 'n some vittles…"

"Wait, who's he?"

"Massa Carter? He owns this farm, but he went to war 'n ain't come back yet."

"Why do you call him 'Master'?"

"Reckon it's 'cause everybody else does, 'cept Missy Carter 'n their chillun. She took 'em all off to Macon when the bluecoat prisoners first started comin' to the stockade."

"And they left you and your mother alone?"

"The field hands ran off when Massa Carter left. Me 'n Momma stayed in the cabin 'cause we ain't got no other place to go. Massa Carter said Momma can leave when he comes back, but he ain't said nothin' 'bout what he gonna do with me." Mr. Frank stares at me with eyes like a fox. He reaches out to put 'is hand on my head. I want 'im to touch me, but I draw back right quick.

"I forgot, Joe. I shouldn't leave my scent on you. But, I'm very confused. Are you saying your mother is Mr. Carter's slave?"

"She don't like that word, but she b'longs to Massa Carter all right."

"Then you must be a slave…I mean, belong to him too."

"That's what folk say."

"But, you're not…I mean your skin is white and your eyes are light." He keeps on starin' at me like I got pox.

"I reckon I ain't old 'nough to know 'bout them things, 'least that's what Momma says. The white chillun at the camp shy 'way from me, sometimes they pick at me. Field hands' chillun don't play with me, 'fraid I'm hexed by a voodoo woman over in the swamp. I figure I'm too white to be colored 'n too colored to be white. Maybe when I grow up I'll turn one color or the other, find me a real name, 'n have more friends 'sides jist Tater 'n Ben."

"Your real name's not Joe?"

"It is, but I ain't got a family name to go with it."

"And your mother?"

"She's jist Della 'n that's all."

"Are you forgetting you're my *niji*?"

"But you're a bluecoat. You gonna light out from these woods real soon." I wait a minute to see if he's gonna change 'is mind 'bout leavin'. No sign he'll stay. "Anyway, I gotta git goin' 'fore Momma comes after me with 'er washin' paddle. Come on, Tater, let's go hitch Ben 'n peddle peanuts."

"Joe, remember that *nijis* might separate, but they're never far apart." Mr. Frank's curious words rattle 'round my head all the way to the cabin.

7

I stop by the barn to string tie the rabbit 'fore takin' it to Momma.

"Lordy, Lordy," Momma squeals when I hand over the wigglin' rabbit. "How in the world did you catch it?" The first thing outta her mouth's a question I don't wanna answer. Ever since that bluecoat injun came 'long, it's gittin' harder 'n harder to tell the truth without sayin' what my eyes really see.

"Uhh...I found it by the creek, Momma."

"Found it? Is it sick?"

"No'm. Got its leg caught 'n couldn't get loose. I brought it back to the cabin for supper."

Momma raises 'er eyebrows 'n grumbles, "Um, huh," like she knows I slacked off on the truth a little. "The good Lord looks after fools 'n sinners. I know better'n to doubt the works o' the Lord, but thank you Lord for sendin' this po' critter our way."

She goes out 'hind the corncrib to dress the rabbit with Tater at 'er heels. He knows Momma's gonna let 'im feast on some leavin's. While she's busy, I hitch Ben to the cart 'n head over to the camp with my big sack o' peanuts. 'Fore takin' off, I sneak back 'n drop a pinch o' tobacco...uh, *kinikinic* on the rabbit's blood.

The camp's buzzin' like a hornet's nest today. Ben acts skittish 'n bucks the traces. Strange things're goin' on like I never seen. Guards run 'round 'n holler orders to black men in bluecoat uniforms. They're haulin' firewood to stoke the train engine at the depot. Other guards load prisoners on the cattle cars like they're headin' off from Camp Sumter. Field hands dig in the hard red clay at the edge o' camp, more'n I ever seen workin' at one time.

"Look out, boy!" a man hollers as his mule team nearly runs me down. The mules haul a big cannon over to where the field hands're pilin' dirt.

BOOM! Another cannon goes off from 'cross the stockade 'n scares the breath outta me. Women scream, horses rear up 'n men let go words that I'd get whupped for sayin'. I've heard that cannon after sundown b'fore, but never this close. Mr. Dukes says it reminds the prisoners they ain't got no chance to 'scape. The time don't seem right for peddlin' peanuts, so I turn Ben 'round 'n start back towards the scary road through the woods.

A guard on a lathered horse rides up 'n hollers, "Go back, boy, Yankees are coming!" I don't know if he means prisoners or the Union army. A string o' wagons follow, headin' into camp full o' all kinds o' folk—old men, women, chillun, some black 'n some white. Me 'n Ben, curious 'bout the strange goin's on, turn back 'n follow the last wagon to the store.

There ain't no place at the store for my cart, so I lead Ben back to a post near the blacksmith shop. With the sack o' peanuts over my shoulder, I make my way through the crowd o' people— all standin' 'round talkin' like crows in a cornfield. Some o' the guards see me, but they're too busy to buy goobers. I see it ain't jist the reserves on the stockade pigeon roosts with rifles—they're all totin' guns. I mosey over to the store 'n stand 'round starin' at the sky like I ain't listenin' to what folks say.

"Yankee cavalry's headed to Anderson Station to turn prisoners loose," one guard hollers.

Another guard tells Mr. Dukes, "Capt'n Wirtz is sending all able-bodied bluecoats to another prison so they can't help the raiders." Folk pour into camp from all 'round to hide from the Yankees, even some from Alabama.

"The whole Union Army's headed this way from the northwest through Columbus and they might burn Oglethorpe on the way," a farmer hollers as he cuts 'is wagon through the crowd. My ears perk up. Massa Carter's farm sets on the Oglethorpe Road north o' camp. Momma might be in harm's way.

I take off runnin' to untie Ben so I can tell Momma the war's comin' to Anderson Station. Workin' my way through the crowd with my head down I bump into one o' the guards.

"What's yo' hurry there, Goober boy?" It's Corporal Jake Tolliver, the meanest man in gray britches. He grabs my galluses 'n pulls my face close to his. His breath smells worse than donkey dung. "You high tailin' off to join up with yo' Yankee buddies? Maybe you ain't heard what Yankee raiders do to half-breeds like you. They stick their swords in yo' gut 'n rip right up to yo' neck." He sticks the barrel o' the gun in my stomach.

"N-n-no suh, Mr. Jake, I ain't runnin' off." I can tell by the corporal's beady eyes it won't take much for 'im to shoot me dead. There ain't nobody to help me. Everybody's studyin' what they gonna do 'bout the Yankees. I'm on my own with this bully breathin' in my face. It comes to mind he's crazy 'bout peanuts.

"Mr. Jake, I'm jist headin' over to the blacksmith shed to water my donkey. Maybe you won't mind tendin' to my sack o' peanuts 'til I come back?"

He loosens 'is grip. "Now, how do I know these goobers is fittin' to eat?" He leans the rifle 'gainst 'is leg 'n puts 'is hand out. A crooked grin crawls 'cross his lips. "Gimme some to inspect." I look down at 'is hand holdin' my galluses. He turns loose to let me set the sack down. I scoop out a double handful o' peanuts. He cracks the peanuts 'n gobbles 'em down wastin' time—time I need to warn Momma 'bout the Yankees comin'. Gotta think quick.

"Mr. Jake, I'll mosey on over 'n water my donkey. If anybody wants to buy peanuts while I'm gone, 'member they go for a token a bunch." Them beady eyes shine like new dollars.

Headin' for the blacksmith shed, I figure losin' my poke o' peanuts is more'n a fair trade for Momma's life.

Leavin' the camp without Corporal Tolliver spottin' me won't be easy. The road's packed with folks comin' in, not goin' out. I untie Ben 'n wait. Soon a guard leads some bluecoat parolees towards the woods, packin' saws 'n axes. So I pull Ben right up b'side 'em.

"Hey, boy, where're you going with that baby wagon?" somebody hollers behind me. Actin' like I don't hear, I cluck my tongue for Ben to go faster.

"Lemme borrow your cart for a while," somebody else cries out.

"Leave that boy alone!" I look over my shoulder 'n see a guard who always buys my peanuts. "Hey, Goober Joe, get away from these Yankees before they take your wagon and escape."

"Yessuh." Nothin' I wanna do more'n move on down the road to the spooky woods out o' Corporal Tolliver's sight. Once we cross the creek, I hop on the cart 'n swat Ben on the rump to make him trot me all the way to the farm.

I start to holler 'fore Ben even pulls 'round the big house. "Momma, Momma!" She looks up from 'er boilin' wash pot, but pays me no mind. Ben heads for the barn like always without slowin' down. I jump off the cart. No use a'wastin' time tryin' to show that stubborn jackass who's boss.

"Momma, you gotta go to the camp, the Yankees are comin'!"

"What you sayin' chile?" She backs 'way from the steamin' pot 'n wipes the sweat off 'er face with the apron.

"Yankees're comin', folks're going to Camp Sumter to hide, the guards got cannons out, prisoners're leavin' the stockade, 'n..." My breath gives out.

Momma acts like I ain't said nothin'. "How many tokens'd you take in today, Joe? You ain't been gone long 'nough to sell nothin'."

"Ain't nobody wantin' peanuts today; they all scared o' the Yankees."

"Then bring me some while I finish washin' these bed clothes."

"I ain't got none."

"What! Where they at?"

"That mean corporal what broke our eggs done took 'em 'way from me, the whole sack."

"What did Mr. Dukes say 'bout that?"

"Mr. Dukes got too busy takin' care o' the folks that's runnin' from the Yankees, all the way from Alabama. We gotta hurry to the camp 'fore the Yankees come down on us."

Momma put 'er hands on 'er hips like she's gonna set me straight 'fore she whups me good. "Listen to me, chile. Yankees don't scare me none," she cocks 'er head, "'cept that dead'un by the creek. They fightin' this war for folk like us. They don't mean us no harm. If they come to this place, I'll feed 'em what we got 'n send 'em on their way. If they wanna set prisoners loose, I'll show 'em the way to that swamp they call a prison." She stops to take a breath. "You git on 'bout yo' chores 'fore I have a mind to take this wash paddle to yo' backside. Now git!"

I don't understand why Momma wants the Yankees to come. She never talked that way 'fore now. What if Momma don't know 'bout Yankees cuttin' boys to pieces with their swords? I wanna ask 'er 'bout bein' a half-breed, but she ain't in no mood for questions. Mr. Frank can set me straight 'bout Yankees, even if he is the injun kind.

I unhitch Ben from the cart 'n mess 'round the barn 'til Momma starts hangin' out the wash. Then I slip through the big house cellar 'n climb upstairs to Massa Carter's room. I pull back a curtain to let the light in 'n open the cabinet to get Mr. Frank some clothes. Massa Carter don't wear no overalls, so a pair o' pantaloons 'n a gray shirt'll have to do for my *niji*.

Horses come gallopin' toward the house. It's probably Corporal Tolliver comin' after me. I ease over to the window 'n see two men on horses. They ain't wearin' guard uniforms. I wonder if Corporal Tolliver sent 'em after me for runnin' off? I'd best get back to the cellar 'n crack the door to hear what they're tellin' Momma.

"Della, we got word the Yankee raiders're on their way to Camp Sumter to set the prisoners loose. They're burning everything in sight. Captain Wirtz wants everybody to load up with provisions and go on over to the camp."

"Yessuh," Momma says in her way of agreein' with somethin' she don't believe.

"Fine, we'll be on our way and see you at the camp." The man doin' the talkin' owns a big plantation jist up the road towards Oglethorpe. They ride off 'n Momma goes back to the clothesline. I come out o' the cellar, hide the clothes in the barn 'n go to the kitchen for somethin' to feed Mr. Frank. The rabbit's soakin' in brine on the stove, not cooked yet. There's always cornbread in the oven. I break off a piece for Mr. Frank 'n stuff it in my back pocket.

Momma comes to the kitchen. "You hungry, Joe? I'll fix us some dinner." When she opens the oven door, I start talkin', hopin' she won't notice the hunk o' cornbread I took.

"Momma, are we goin' to the camp?"

She shakes 'er head 'n slides the pan o' cornbread outta the oven. "Uh humm, looks like somebody in this room done got somethin' to eat." She cuts 'er eyes 'round at me.

"Yessum." I duck my head to shut out that look I hate.

"Joe, I know you growin' like willows on the creek, but you ain't got no cause to slip 'round 'n take vittles outta the kitchen. Since you done ate already, go make yo'self handy. There's more to do 'round this place than a body can shake a stick at."

"Yessum." She don't hafta to tell me 'gain to get out o' her sight. From the kitchen she won't see me slip out the other side o' the barn with Massa Carter's clothes stuffed under my overalls. I cut through the orchard 'n pick some cider apples. They ain't ripe yet, but they'll do for now. Comin' close to the creek I holler so

Mr. Frank'll know it's me 'n won't bother to hide. Tater crosses the creek 'head o' me 'n runs right up to Mr. Frank hunkered down in the shade.

"*Boozhoo* Joe," he says raisin' 'is hand high. I'm struck dumb by what he says 'n what I see—no shirt, a band o' swamp grass wrapped 'round 'is head 'n some feathers in 'is other hand. His skin, darker'n mine, is the color o' field dirt. My eyes 'bout pop outta my head 'n my tongue rolls into a knot.

"That's an Ojibwe greeting. I didn't expect you so soon. Is something wrong?"

I nod my head, tryin' to untie my tongue. "I reckon so, Yankee army's headin' this way."

Mr. Frank jumps up 'n puts 'is hand on my shoulder. "How do you know?" I reckon it don't matter if his scent gits on me now, 'cause the Yankees're comin' to take over the camp.

"Folks at the camp're talkin'."

"Hmm…tell me exactly what you heard, Joe."

"I can't 'member all of it. The Yankee cavalry's comin' over from Alabama to set the prisoners free. All the folk 'round're movin' to the camp. Camp guards're totin' guns 'n they pulled out more cannons. Some say fightin''ll start today, some say tomorrow."

Mr. Frank pats me on the shoulder 'n walks over to a sunny spot by the creek. Clearin' 'way pine straw, he pushes a stick in the ground 'n runs a finger 'long the stick's short shadow.

"That is north," he says pointin' upstream. He stands straight as a board lookin' at the sky over the creek. Liftin' the feathers 'bove his head, he starts to hum. Then he lowers the feathers, changin' the hummin' to grunts. His feet move like he's walkin', but he don't go nowhere. Suddenly, he stops, lifts his chin high like he's waitin' for somethin' or somebody to answer 'is crazy song.

The quiet makes my scalp tingle. "I brought you some clothes 'n cornbread." He lifts 'is hand for me to be quiet. I pull Massa Carter's pantaloons 'n shirt from under my overalls 'n lay 'em with the cornbread on the pine straw at my feet. What is this injun Yankee up to? Maybe he's tryin' to figure out what to do with me now that his own army's a comin'. Maybe he's gonna use 'is sharp piece o' tin to cut me open like Corporal Tolliver said. I can't stay 'n git cut open. Pullin' Tater back from the cornbread, I take off sloshin' 'cross the creek.

"Wait!" Mr. Frank hollers. My mind tells me to run for my life, but my feet won't go. "Thanks for bringing the clothes 'n food." I nod my head. "Are you and your mother going to the camp?"

"She won't go. She ain't 'fraid o' Yankees. She says when they come; she'll feed'em 'n show'em the way to the prison. Do you think she's crazy?"

"Are you crazy for helping me?" Mr. Frank forgets his injun ways and talks normal again. My skin stops tinglin'.

"Corporal Tolliver says Yankees cut open half-breeds like me with their swords."

The big Yankee injun laughs. "That's what someone told my boys about Confederate soldiers." He stoops down, cups 'is hands 'n drinks from the creek. He wipes 'is hands on 'is pants. "Is that what the corporal calls you or is it what you call yourself?"

"What?"

"Half-breed."

"He calls me half-breed, but I don't know what it means."

"Did you ever ask your mother?"

"One time, but she got mad 'n told me to pay no 'tention to what people call me. She said my name's Joe 'n that's all I need to know." Mr. Frank motions me to come back 'cross the creek 'n set with 'im. I ain't 'fraid no more. He breaks the cornbread 'n hands me a piece. I pull a green apple outta my pocket 'n give it to 'im.

"You make a good Indian, Joe. Never receive a gift without offering something in return." He takes a bite o' the apple.

"If you had a father, he'd tell you stories about who you are, like this story I told my children: Many years ago, a Frenchman named François came to a big lake called *Kitchi Gami* to trap

beaver and sell their furs. There he met an Ojibwe princess and
they were married. When beaver furs became scarce many of the
trappers moved west but François remained behind to raise his
family. Soon a son was born. Half his blood was French and half
was Ojibwe. Some trappers called François' son *bois brulé,* which
in English means 'half-burnt wood'. Others used a kinder word,
métis, for children of mixed race parents."

Mr. Frank stops to take a bite o' cornbread 'n goes to the
creek for water to wash it down b'fore tellin' the rest of the story:
"François chose to raise his son in the ways of the Ojibwe because
the tribe treated *métis* children with great respect. François was
very proud of his son. When the son grew to manhood he earned
an Ojibwe name, *Eagle-with-Three-Tongues.* "

"Three tongues?"

"Yes, because he spoke three languages, Ojibwe, English and
French."

"What was his family name?"

"He was François Beauregard, Jr. to the French but the
English called him Frank." Mr. Frank grins, waitin' for me to
catch on to the story 'bout his life.

"So you're not a real injun are you?"

"As real as the sunrise, Joe. Mixed blood doesn't make you
any less real. Your mother's right. Don't listen to the names other
people call you, listen to the voice inside your heart."

"Then I must be a 'mayteese' like you, Mr. Frank." I jump to
my feet feelin' a little taller 'n a lot smarter. I give Tater the last
bite o' my cornbread 'n leave the Eagle-with-Three-Tongues to go
on with his injun singin'. Sure wish I could tell Momma 'bout my
new *niji* I found down by the creek. I pull up some tall grass on
the way to the cabin to make me a headband like the one Mr. Frank
wears.

8

Next mornin' the sun comes up like thunder. Cannons blastin' from Camp Sumter roust me from a deep sleep. I slip on my overalls 'n run to the porch. Momma hollers for me to come back inside the cabin.

"I ain't goin' nowhere, jist wanna see if any Yankees come yet."

She rambles to the door in 'er nightgown 'n stretches 'er light brown arms high. "Well, I don't see no Yankees 'round here," she laughs. "Go fetch some stove wood so I can fix breakfast." A train whistle cuts through the heavy mornin' air like three wails from a bobcat in pain.

"Yankees ain't come to the camp yet, either. That train won't pull out if they's fightin'," Momma says. The train puffs hard headin' our way from the depot. I wanna run to the crossin' 'n wave at the engineer, but stove wood don't git to the kitchen by itself. I fetch the wood 'n drop one piece at a time in the box by the stove.

Momma notices me messin' 'round with the wood. "Somethin' on yo' mind, Joe?"

"Jist thinkin' 'bout what that guard called me yesterday."

"Umm huh." She lifts a cover-plate from the stove 'n points at the hole.

I shove three sticks o' wood through the openin' 'n watch the sleepy coals turn to flames. "He called me that name you don't like."

She slams the iron cover over the hole 'n shakes her head. "Uh uh uh." I wait for a sign to keep on talkin'. "He called you what?"

"Half-breed."

Momma slides the iron skillet over the eye, slips in a chunk o' lard 'n moves it 'round with a wood spoon. She hands me the egg basket off the shelf. "Here, scoot out to the barn 'n bring me some eggs while the pan heats up. Don't leave any for the foxes." I don't know if she's done talkin' 'bout "half-breed" or jist makin' time to think.

The hens squawk 'n flutter through the barn fussin' at me f'r stealin' eggs outta their nests. I run back to the kitchen 'n set the basket on the table. Momma takes two brown eggs outta the basket 'n cracks 'em in the skillet.

"What'd I tell you 'bout folks callin' you names?" she says, stirrin' the eggs.

"Pay 'em no mind."

"So, don't bother askin' yo' momma questions not fittin' to answer." She scrapes scrambled eggs out o' the skillet on our plates.

"But Momma, don't 'half-breed' mean I got mixed blood in me? That ain't bad...is it?"

"Won't kill you chile. Who tol' you that?"

"Jist heard it from nobody in pa'tic'lar."

She unwraps warm hoecakes from a cloth, drops one on each plate 'n takes 'er seat at the table 'cross from me. "Yo' blood won't kill you but bein' too curious will."

She reaches over, takes my hands in hers 'n bows 'er head. "Lord, you done been too good to us. You done give us gracious plenty to eat 'n a roof over our heads. I thank you 'n my Joe thanks you too. Keep yo' blessin's comin' 'n clean out Joe's mind o' that trash folk done put in it. Amen." After she puts my worry in the hands o' the Lord, Momma folds some egg in the hoecake 'n takes a bite.

Breakfast done, gotta make haste with my chores so I can talk to Mr. Frank. After feedin' the stock 'n milkin', I rake up the wash pot ashes 'n dump 'em in the potash frame for Momma to make soap. A low rumble comes outta the west.

"Momma, Momma, I hear the Yankee cannons." Momma comes out to the back stoop. She laughs 'n goes back to the kitchen. I follow her 'n ask, "Why you laughin'?"

"I reckon you ain't looked at the sky 'fore you hollered. The Lord's gonna send rain to keep the corn from parchin' on the stalks. You ain't seen them worrisome clouds risin' over the trees—it's a fixin' to blow hard. Go close the hayloft door 'n fasten everythin' good 'n tight."

Momma ain't the only one knowin' a storm's 'bout to blow. The cows 'n mules bunch up at the gate rantin' to git in the barn. I open a stall gate 'n 'nother brown egg's starin' me in the face.

"Look, Tater, breakfast for Mr. Frank! My *niji's* mighty hungry—Momma'll never know. Let's go tell 'im 'bout the storm." After the barn's shut up tight, me 'n Tater take off towards the creek. Another rumble o' thunder rolls in from the west.

"Mr. Frank, Mr. Frank," I holler, crossin' the creek. Tater runs to the spot where we found 'im b'fore, but he ain't there. Tater takes off sniffin' up the creek bed past the big blackberry patch. He finds Mr. Frank bendin' saplin's over. "Mr. Frank, a big storm's a comin'," I holler.

"*Boozhoo*, little *métis niji.* You see; I'm preparing for falling water."

"Oh! You're makin' a shelter!" How dumb I feel, tellin' this injun it's a fixin' to rain.

"Not easy without tools, but it's better than my *shebang* in the stockade. Here, hold these saplings while I lash them together." He wraps strips o' willow bark 'round the tips o' the bent gum trees. "Now, help me break off some pine limbs that'll shed water." We finish coverin' the shelter 'n crawl inside to try it out for size. "It's not birch bark, Joe, but I think it'll keep me dry."

"I brought you one egg to eat, but don't know how you gonna cook it. I didn't bring no matches."

He takes the egg 'n looks it over. "Thank you, Joe, no need to cook it." He breaks off a thin gum stem, pokes a hole in the end o' the egg 'n holds it over 'is head. Then he whispers some injun words 'n sucks the egg 'til he slurps air. "Ahhh, I could eat a dozen like this, but I'm grateful for one."

"Foxes suck eggs too, but I reckon you already know that."

"Yes, *Gitchi Manito* gave animals much knowledge and we can learn from them."

I'd heard that word before. "What's *Gitchi Manito*?"

"One who created *Anishinabe*, the original Ojibwe."

"Momma says the Lord done that."

Mr. Frank looks at me with soft eyes. He puts 'is hand on my shoulder 'n says, "Each tribe that walks the earth has its own name for The Great Spirit, but not all hear the Spirit with the same ears."

This Eagle-with-Three-Tongues talks with one tongue that ain't makin' sense. "I don't know what you're sayin', Mr. Frank."

"You will one day, Joe. *Manitos* are spirits in the creatures, in the plants, in all of creation around us. Listen and they will teach you respect for our Mother Earth, for all people, all creatures, all plants and lead you along the good path of life."

"Will they give me 'nother name?"

"That depends on how well you learn from the Mother Earth. Now I must gather more straw for my *wigiwam* before the rain comes."

"Wigiwam?"

"My new shelter in the woods." Thunder rumbles a little louder, a little closer. "And you need to return to your own house."

"Come on, Tater, let's git to the cabin." As Tater scrambles outta Mr. Frank's shelter, I notice Massa Carter's clothes tucked in the shadow of the back wall. "Do the clothes fit?"

Mr. Frank picks up the shirt 'n pantaloons. "Take them back where you got them." He folds 'n stuffs 'em under my overalls bib. "The Union soldiers may mistake me for Johnny Reb if I'm not in uniform. If the camp guards see me in that outfit, they'll shoot me for a spy. I have no choice, Joe. Besides, you'll get into trouble for aiding an escaped prisoner."

He walks with me far as the creek. "Last night I tried to make a band for my head like yours, Mr. Frank, but it didn't work."

"It takes a while to learn. Next time you come I'll show you how." He takes off 'is band o' grass 'n gives it to me. "Here, take mine—one headband for one egg—fair trade." I slip it over my head but it sets on my ears. He smiles. "Don't worry; your head will grow with wisdom."

A clap of thunder shakes the ground. Mr. Frank holds up 'is hand 'n moves it back 'n forth like he's countin'.

"Five thousand meters, I'd say. Rain's about an hour away." Then a cannon blast rips the air. "Sounds like Captain Wirtz is testing his old artillery for battle. You'd better run, Joe. It won't do to get caught between a storm and Union cavalry."

As I run through the cornfield, the wind picks up, whippin' leaves 'gainst my face. Tater runs 'head o' me barkin'. I come out o' the cornfield to the peanut patch 'n see a guard standin' in the yard holdin' a rifle. Momma's on the porch wavin' 'er arms like she's talkin'. I ease back 'tween the cornstalks 'n make my way towards the barn hopin' they won't see me. I squat down in the open pasture to crawl over to the barn. A blast o' wind catches the headband, liftin' it off my head. When I double back to fetch it, that squeaky barn-door voice I hate cuts through the air.

"Where you been goober boy?" Corporal Tolliver trots out o' the barn holdin' a rifle in one hand 'n my empty peanut sack in t'other. "Been lookin' for you boy." Momma follows a few steps b'hind 'im with worry on 'er face. When the corporal gits close he breaks a wicked smile, showin' 'is crooked teeth 'n wavin' the sack in my face.

"Hey boy, you left yo' sack at the camp. I brung it back to you." I reach for the sack, but he pulls it back 'n throws it in the dirt. "Hey, what you got there, boy?" He snatches the headband outta my hand. "Looks like a head piece them Yankee injuns wear at the stockade. Where'd you get this, boy?"

"I...I, er, made it." He raises the rifle 'n points it at the hump in my overalls bib.

"Uh huh, and whacha got tucked under yo' overalls?" He catches Massa Carter's shirt collar with the gun barrel 'n jerks it out. The pantaloons fall at my feet. Momma whimpers 'n covers 'er mouth as the corporal waves the white shirt over me like a flag.

Corporal Tolliver drops the rifle stock to the ground, leans it 'gainst his leg 'n spreads the shirt 'cross my chest. "Looks like this shirt's too big for you boy, whose is it?" I shrug my shoulders 'n look down like Momma told me to do when white folk ask questions. "Pick up them pantaloons boy 'n hold'em to yo' waist." I take my time doin' what he says. "Reckon they don't fit neither. Who'd you steal 'em from...sutler Dukes?"

Tolliver huffs 'cause I don't answer 'n he swats me upside the head with his fist so hard my legs wobble. But I don't fall.

Momma can't hold back no longer, she turns 'n fusses at me to keep from talkin' back to the crazy guard. "What'd you do with the rest o' my washin', Joe? Now take Massa Carter's clothes 'n put 'em with the rest o' the wash."

"Yessum." Momma's eyes burn like fire, tryin' to cover my sin. I fold the pantaloons 'n reach for the shirt in Corporal Tolliver's hand.

"Hold up there, boy. You ain't goin' no where 'cept with me. We gonna take these clothes over to see if you stole 'em from the store." The corporal lifts the rifle 'n acts like he's gonna whop me with the barrel.

"Please don't take my boy, suh, he ain't done nothin'.
Them's Massa Carter's things I been keepin' clean 'til he comes
home." Corporal Tolliver pays Momma no mind. Then he shoves
me so hard I fall at 'er feet. She helps me up, beggin' 'im to let me
go.

"Back off from my prisoner, gal. He ran off yesterday,
'gainst my direct order to stay in camp. I'm takin' 'im to Capt'n
Wirtz. He might wanna put this rascal in stocks."

Momma wraps 'er arms 'round 'er waist 'n walks through the
barn 'head of us. Then she turns 'n faces Corporal Tolliver,
smilin', showin' all 'er teeth. "It's a comin' up a storm, suh.
Come over to the cabin 'n let me fix you somethin' good t'eat.
You gotta be mighty hungry." The corporal stops 'n glances at the
wall o' dark clouds hangin' over the cabin. "We got fresh peas,
poke greens, ham hocks 'n apple pie, won't take long to fix." I
know Momma ain't tellin' the truth 'cause she's grinnin' like she
jist took a bite o' green persimmon. I hope the corporal don't read
'er like I do. Jist then lightenin' flashes over the corn crib 'n a gust
o' wind blows a bunch o' hay outta the barn.

"Reckon I can wait 'til the storm blows over. You say you
got ham hocks?"

"Yessuh," Momma says. "Come over 'n rest on the porch
while I poke up the fire in the stove. Joe, you run pick some
apples for the pie. Hurry 'fore the rain comes."

"Hold on there," growls the corporal, grabbin' my arm.

Momma says, "Don't worry, suh, the orchard's right over
there by the corn crib. You can watch 'im from the porch. He
ain't gonna run to the woods down by the creek with it a comin' up
a storm." She looks me straight in the eye. "Now go 'n act like
you heah yo' momma 'fore I take the wash paddle to yo'
backside." She steps 'tween me 'n Corporal Tolliver so I can take
off to the orchard.

Lightenin' strikes a big pine tree in the woods 'hind the cabin
'n sends up a puff o' white smoke. Ain't nothin' scares me more'n
close-up lightenin'—'cept lookin' down the barrel o' Tolliver's

gun. I reach up to pick the first apple 'n Momma's words ring clear in my head: *He ain't gonna run off to the woods down by the creek!* I look back 'n see Tolliver pointin' that rifle at me 'n realize she means for me to run for my life. I drop the apple, stoop over like I'm gonna pick it up 'n take off runnin' fast as I can, 'way from the house. A shot rings out scarin' the life outta me, but I ain't hit. I keep on runnin', not darin' to look back at the corporal tryin' to kill me.

The bottom falls outta the clouds. The wind blows rain sideways, coverin' my 'scape but makin' it hard to see more'n three steps in front o' me. I cross over the creek that's risin' awful fast. When I git close to Mr. Frank's shelter, I holler to let 'im know I'm comin'.

"Who-eee, Mr. Frank, Mr. Frank, it's Joe." Hopin' he knows it's me, I fall inside the shelter.

Mr. Frank grabs my throat 'fore he sees who I am. "Joe, you gave me a scare. What are you doing here?" He pulls me closer, 'way from the drivin' rain. I can't answer—I'm shakin' all over from being wet, cold, plumb give out 'n scared half to death. Mr. Frank wipes the water from my face 'n holds me close 'til I catch my breath.

"He's comin' after me with a gun, shootin' like crazy."

"Hold on, Joe. Who's chasing you with a gun?" Mr. Frank looks out towards the creek.

"Corporal Tolliver."

"Did he see where you went?"

"I don't think so, 'least I couldn't see him. Anyway, I didn't come d'rectly down here. I went b'hind the cabin 'n doubled back."

"Good thinking. He'll wait for the rain to let up before tracking you down. When he comes, he'll be sorry he found you." Mr. Frank pulls out 'is sharp piece o' tin 'n rubs 'is thumb over the edge.

The rain pounds hard 'n the wind rattles the shelter.

"Don't worry, Joe, it'll hold."

The wind finally dies down as night settles in, but the rain keeps comin' loud 'n heavy. We set still, watchin' 'n listenin' for the crazy corporal to come after me with killin' on 'is mind.

9

Daylight wakes me 'n the rain's stopped. Mr. Frank's settin' straight-backed with eyes wide open.

"Good morning, Joe. The storm's over and has left its footprints in the creek." He moves out o' the shelter 'n stretches 'is arms towards the creek. "Don't worry about the corporal finding you today, look!" Water roars through the bushes like a chargin' bull.

"Creek's never been this high."

"When I was in the stockade we wished for big heavy rainstorms to clean out the sinks."

"The sinks?"

"A long latrine at one end of Stockade Creek, real messy and foul smelling."

"Y'all didn't have no outhouses?"

Mr. Frank steps into the sunlight to dry out. "If I had known the Rebs would pack me off to a big outhouse with no shelter, and trash for food, I would not have let them capture me. A bullet in the head would've been much kinder than rotting in that Confederate cesspool."

I move over close to Mr. Frank's sunny spot. Hearin' 'bout the prison stockade makes me shudder, but I feel safe standin' by him with the sun warmin' my face. This good feelin' leaves me d'rectly. I shouldn't o' run off 'n left Momma at the cabin with that devil, Corporal Tolliver.

"Mr. Frank, I gotta go back 'n see if Momma's all right. Corporal Tolliver might o' put 'er in prison for lettin' me 'scape."

"There's no going back until the water settles down. What'll you do if the corporal's waiting for you?"

"Reckon I'll do what he says 'n let 'im take me back to camp. Momma won't let nothin' bad happen to me. She'll talk to Mr. Dukes 'n Capt'n Wirtz."

"Some of those reserve guards aren't real soldiers, just kids with itchy trigger fingers. That corporal might shoot you on sight."

"Maybe he went on back to camp last night like Momma figgered when she tol' me to run off."

Mr. Frank looks up 'n down the creek. "How do you plan to cross these rapids? You'll either drown or wash down to the stockade."

I think 'bout 'is question, tryin' to 'member how the creek runs through the farm. "The field hands built a rock ford up b'hind the cabin to make a fishin' hole. It makes a good crossin'."

"You don't think it washed away in the flood?"

"Don't know. It's been there since I was little."

"All right, let's go see. You lead the way." The high water covers the trails 'long the creek bed, so I try to find a different way to go upstream. I don't go far 'til the vines 'n brush're too tangled 'n thick to git through.

"Joe, going this way is too rough. Where's the house located from this point?"

"The sun comes up over the camp, so the house oughta be that way." I face the sun 'n raise my left arm.

"North," he says. He turns the opposite direction 'n starts walkin' 'way from the house. I don't say a word—he's the injun; I'm jist a dumb farm boy. We come to a rise in the piney woods where pines're so thick bushes don't grow.

"There, that's better," he says. "We'll follow this ridge, keeping the creek water in view 'til we reach that ford." Walkin's easier, but soon I don't see the creek.

We keep goin' 'til Mr. Frank stops 'n points down the hill.
"The ford is there."

"Where? I don't see nothin' but scrub trees 'n blackberry
vines."

"Try using your ears, Joe. Listen! Hear that? That's either
the ford or a waterfall in that little gorge."

"There ain't no waterfall on this creek."

"Then, let's go down to the ford." We slip 'n slide down the
steep bank 'til we come to a rock dam with water gushin' through
one end that's busted. "Looks like most of the ford held up under
the flood. I'll help you across the break. Can you scale the hill
and find your way from there?"

"I've done it 'fore, tho' Momma says it's too dangerous 'n
full o' snakes."

Mr. Frank straddles the break 'n holds my hand as I jump
over to the ford. A shallow stream o' water flows over the top.
Every step I take feels like I'm gonna wash over 'n fall in the mad
waters under me. Holdin' my breath, I make it to the other side 'n
grab a saplin'.

"Good job, Joe," Mr. Frank hollers. "Now be careful when
you get there. Remember you're dealing with a wild animal and
he won't hesitate to hurt you without cause."

I start up the trail to the house 'n turn back to wave at my *niji*
who's still straddlin' the break. My feet slip 'n slide up the steep
hill leadin' to the springhouse. At the top, I catch my breath 'n
heah the cows lowin', waitin' to be milked 'n let out to pasture. I
don't see no smoke comin' outta the chimney, I reckon Momma
didn't cook no breakfast. I whistle for Tater, but he don't come.

I ease over to the back stoop 'n listen. Ain't nothin' movin'
in the cabin. The kitchen's cold, ain't no fire in the stove. I crack
open the front door 'n peep out to see if Corporal Tolliver's still
lookin' for me. Ain't nobody on the porch. Somethin' on the wet
porch floor catches my eye—it's a dark spot. I look closer. Could
it be...? It is blood!

"Momma!" I scream loud as I can, forgettin' the corporal might be hidin', waitin' for me. I jump off the porch 'n run to the barn, lookin' everywhere. "Ben, where's Momma, where's Tater? I wish you could talk."

I race back to the cabin to look. She still ain't here. I holler one mo' time, "Momma, Momma, where are you?"

"Joe?" A voice calls me from b'hind the house, but it ain't Momma. My heart stops—then I realize it ain't Corporal Tolliver, it's Mr. Frank. I rush to the back stoop 'n find 'im standin' in the springhouse shadow.

"Momma's gone 'n blood's all over the front porch," I holler. Mr. Frank looks 'round 'fore he comes 'cross the yard to meet me.

"Easy, Joe, easy, keep your voice low. I heard you scream and came from the creek fast as I could. Are you sure nobody's here?"

"Just chickens 'n cows 'n pigs 'n mules 'n…"

"Whoa, I mean people. Let's have a look. Maybe the animals can tell us something." I follow 'im through the cabin, thinkin' he might be some kind o' spirit after all. He looks at the blood-splattered porch.

"Somebody got shot all right," he says, "but not with a rifle. A shotgun made this mess." I step back inside 'n look for Massa Carter's shotgun under Momma's mattress.

"It ain't here!"

"What?"

"Nothin'," I ain't s'posed to talk 'bout the shotgun.

Mr. Frank steps off the porch, sloshes through the mud with 'is head down 'n stops at the barn door. "Somebody left the barn door open in that storm last night," he says pointin' to the damp hay coverin' the floor.

"I shut that door 'fore I ran off."

Mr. Frank goes over to Ben's stall 'n lifts the latch. "What do you know about all this, my little brother with big ears?" He strokes Ben's stiff mane 'n steps back to let 'im out. Ben nuzzles me 'n moves to the stall stacked with bales o' hay. He presses 'is head 'gainst the stall gate 'n won't move.

"Well," says Mr. Frank. "Let's see what's bothering you." He pulls Ben back 'n opens the gate. Then he squats down 'n brushes back some loose hay on the floor. "Joe, step back. I'm going to lift one of the bales and have a look. There may be something here you don't need to see."

I move back from the stall 'n stand by Ben. Mr. Frank rolls the top bale over, then puts it back. He comes outta the stall 'n latches the gate. "Joe, I hate to tell you this...There's a body under the hay."

"Momma?"

"No, it's a man, a Johnny Reb."

My mouth turns to cotton. I put Ben back in 'is stall 'n make myself swallow so I can talk. "Who is it?"

"Don't know, but there're two stripes on his sleeve."

"Corporal Tolliver?"

"Likely."

"We got a poke o' trouble, Mr. Frank."

"Likely," he says 'gain.

A dog barks far off. I rush outside to listen...ain't no bloodhound...might be Tater. A spot o' orange bounces outta the cornfield runnin' towards me.

"Come 'ere, Tater dog. Where you...?" Another body comes through the cornstalks 'n makes my heart jump outta my chest.

"Joe," Momma screams. She comes closer, holdin' the shotgun up high. I run to meet 'er in the peanut patch. She drops the gun 'n wraps 'er arms 'round me so tight I can't breathe.

"I been lookin' for you since daylight. I thought you done got drowned in the creek. Oh my boy, you're fine, fine as can be." She starts to cry.

"We're both fine, Momma."

She pushes me back 'n puts on 'er serious face.   "No,   Joe we ain't.   We gotta pack up 'n move out.   Somethin' bad done happened."

"I know Momma, I know."   The words're fresh outta my mouth when she picks up the shotgun 'n aims it towards the barn. Mr. Frank stands in the barn door.

"No, Momma, no, it's Mr. Frank."   She acts like she's gone deaf 'n moves by me with the gun aimed at my *niji*. I run after 'er hollerin', "Don't shoot 'im, don't shoot 'im!"

Mr. Frank raises 'is hands, smilin', not afraid.   "You're Joe's mother?" he asks.

She comes closer.   "Who you be 'n what you doin' in Massa Carter's barn?"

"M'am, I'm Private François Beauregard of the Wisconsin Volunteers. I joined the army to set your people free, but the rebels captured me at the Wilderness last May and sent me to Camp Sumter."   When Mr. Frank stops talkin', I move between him 'n Momma so the shotgun's pointin' at my chest.

"He's a good man, Momma.   He's got a boy like me."

Momma lowers the gun barrel.   Mr. Frank turns the palm of 'is hand towards Momma.   "Pleased to make your acquaintance Mrs…"

"Folk call me Della."   Momma drops 'er head, but keeps 'er eyes on Mr. Frank.   She ain't sure 'bout 'im yet.

"…Mrs. Della.   You have a mighty fine young man.   He worried all night about leaving you alone with…" he jerks 'is head towards the barn, "…that guard."

Momma gasps 'n leans the shotgun 'gainst the barn wall. She puts 'er arms 'round me 'n starts cryin'.   "Lordy, lordy, suh, I didn't aim to kill 'im, but he was 'bout to shoot my boy in the back.   They gonna hang me for sho', if we don't git gone."

Mr. Frank takes the shotgun, pops the other shell out 'n sticks it in 'is pocket.   "Did the guard come here alone?"   Momma nods 'er head 'n keeps on cryin'.   "Then there may be a way out of this situation."

Momma listens to what Mr. Frank says, but the cat's got 'er tongue. My stomach rumbles, catchin' 'er 'tention.

"Lordy me, Joe, I better fix you somethin' t' eat." Startin' towards the cabin, she stops 'n looks back at Mr. Frank. "I reckon they don't feed y'all good at the prison, do they?" Mr. Frank shakes 'is head. "Come in the kitchen while I fix some vittles. Joe, go to the springhouse 'n fetch the milk 'n butter while I put a fire in the stove." I wanna hear Mr. Frank's plan, but this ain't no time to sass my momma.

I hurry back from the springhouse. Momma's put Mr. Frank to work rubbin' lard on the sweet potatoes while they talk. She's still got worry lines 'cross 'er face. "You say Capt'n Wirtz ain't gonna send out nobody lookin' for that corporal?"

Mr. Frank holds up a greased yam for 'er to see. "I think not. The guard probably left his post under ready alert. It's happened before. Those reserves are just kids and old men. They get homesick, leave their units and return weeks later. The regular army considers it desertion, but the rebels are so short handed they turn their backs like it never happened."

Momma nods 'er head 'n rolls out biscuit dough on the breadboard. "What we gonna do 'bout the body in the barn? Can't leave it where I drug it."

"Don't worry. I'll bury it down at the creek next to that cavalryman…"

Momma yips like a dog 'n looks at me with fire in 'er eyes, "What?"

"I didn't tell Mr. Frank nothin'."

"He speaks the truth, Mrs. Della, I figured it out for myself."

"Mr. Frank is injun, Momma. He reads folks' minds."

Momma cuts 'er eyes towards Mr. Frank. "I can tell he ain't white, but readin' minds? I don't know 'bout that." She slips the skillet o' biscuits in the oven. "Tell me, Mr. Frank, what you gonna do after you bury…that man?"

"We have to clean the blood off the porch and burn the hay to remove the corporal's scent from the barn. The storm washed out his tracks and the trail where you dragged him to the barn. When I'm finished there'll be no trace left, so you and Joe can stay here safely."

Momma puts the sweet potatoes in the oven 'n pours buttermilk into fruit jars on the table. "Then what you gonna do?" she asks Mr. Frank. He sips the buttermilk 'n draws 'is lips tight like it might be bad. "Nothin' wrong with it, suh. I reckon they don't have buttermilk where you come from."

Mr. Frank's stomach tells 'im not to argue. He downs the whole jar full 'n wipes 'is shirtsleeve 'cross his mouth. "Tastes like soured milk."

Momma says, "That's what t'is; keeps longer'n sweet milk 'n it's better on yo' stomach."

"You asked about my plans. My only hope is to join with the Union army heading this way. If only I knew where and when..."

"Folk say they comin' from Oglethorpe, maybe tomorrow," I tell 'im. "That road runs right by this farm."

"Mmmm, *Gitchi Manito* smiles on me," Mr. Frank says. Momma closes 'er eyes 'n shakes 'er head.

"That's injun talk for Great Spirit, Momma."

She brightens up, "You mean it's the Holy Spirit?"

Mr. Frank laughs, "Something like that."

Now he's caught Momma's 'tention 'n they start talkin' 'bout spirit things I don't understand. When the biscuits're done, she wraps the apron 'round 'er hand, pulls the skillet out 'n dumps 'em on the breadboard. Then she forks the sweet potatoes outta the pan onto the plates.

"Show Mr. Frank how to fix them yams."

I slice open a sweet potato 'n spread butter over the steamin' orange sweetness.

"Let it cool first, Mr. Frank, or you'll burn the hair off yo' tongue," Momma laughs.

We're all too hungry to talk while we eat. Mr. Frank finishes 'n thanks Momma for the good food. "I should go and take care of the corporal's body. If it's all right with you Mrs. Della, I'll stay one more night in the woods and wait for the army." He stops at the door to look out 'fore leavin'.

Momma calls out, "Wait, Mr. Frank." She goes to the other room to fetch a' old sheet 'n hands it to 'im. "Even a mean man oughta be buried in a proper shroud." Then Momma pulls the cavalryman's letter from 'er dress pocket. "We found this in that soldier's pocket," she says, showin' Mr. Frank the letter. He opens it 'n draws 'is eyes 'cross the paper.

"It's a letter he wrote to his mother. The address is worn off, but it says something about returning to Chippewa Valley. If it's agreeable with you I'll see that the cavalryman's mother gets this when I return to Wisconsin." Momma nods 'er head 'n he slips the letter in 'is pocket. "I'll also tell her where his body's buried in case she wants to recover it after the war."

Momma fights back tears 'n gives me a chore, "Joe, go hitch Ben to the cart so Mr. Frank don't have to tote the body down to the creek. Git the shovels from the shed 'n help 'im dig the grave. Don't forget to say a prayer for the corporal's soul."

"Yessum."

"And Joe, don't you let Mr. Frank stay in the woods. He might not heah the bluecoats when they come. You bring 'im back 'n fix a place in the hayloft." I don't know why she talks to me, since Mr. Frank's standin' right in front o' 'er. I jist know I'm glad he's gonna be close by when the Union Army gits here.

"Yessum." 'Fore headin' to the shed, I whisper to Mr. Frank, "Is the bluecoat's name on the letter?"

"He signed it 'James'."

"What's 'is family name?"

"Doesn't say."

"Oh."

10

We pack the cart with hay 'n Mr. Frank wraps the sheet 'round the corporal's body 'n rifle. A sad feelin' comes over me 'til I 'member how Corporal Tolliver acted like I wan't no better'n the horse dung on the heel o' 'is boot.

"He won't fit, his legs stick out," Mr. Frank says. "Find a long board so his feet won't drag 'n leave a trail."

I look 'round the barn for some loose planks, but there ain't none, jist a piece o' fence. "Will a fence rail do?" I holler.

"Bring it here and we'll see."

He shoves the rail through the hay under the body 'n ties the legs together with twine. Then we cover the body with more hay. I send Tater back to the cabin 'n lead Ben 'cross the pasture to the split-rail fence that runs down to the creek.

I don't hear Mr. Frank's footsteps 'hind me so I look back to make sure he's still there. "Pasture's awful muddy," I holler. No answer, so I ask 'im, "What's yo' boy's name, Mr. Frank?"

Silence.

His face is long 'n he rolls his eyes back 'n forth across the sky like he's searchin' for somethin'. He draws a hand 'cross 'is mouth 'n shakes 'is head slow, a sign to hush. "Umm huh," I grumble under my breath jist like Momma. We follow the rail fence 'til we see the creek. The water's still high, rushin' like a river over its banks. I slip some rails outta the notches on the posts to make a gap for Ben to pull the cart through.

Finally Mr. Frank loosens 'is tongue. "Show me where you and your mother buried the cavalryman?"

"There, water's runnin' over it." Mr. Frank walks to the rise where water laps at 'is boots. He makes sounds in his throat like a screech owl. Then he talks—seems he's tryin' to sing, but can't work up a tune. The words don't make no sense. He must be talkin' to the creek or the man we buried. I know he ain't talkin' to me. It's spooky standin' 'tween the dead man on my cart 'n this injun tryin' to sing, flappin' 'is arms like he's gonna fly. Next Mr. Frank turns 'round 'n steps off three paces from the water.

"We'll dig here, away from the high water." I git the shovels from the cart 'n hand 'im one. He draws lines on the ground like Momma did when we dug the cavalryman's grave, then he pushes the blade deep in the dirt. "Ground's soft from the big rain."

We dig off the topsoil. I can't hold back no longer; my mind's spinnin' like train wheels on wet tracks. "Mr. Frank, did you talk to the creek a while ago?"

He stops to wipe sweat from 'is face 'n looks me in the eye. "I speak to the *Manitos,* not to the water. The cavalryman's body may have washed away in the flood. I asked the *Manitos* to keep him from floating back to the stockade. Tomorrow I'll search for his body and return it to the earth."

I wonder why Mr. Frank 'n Momma take on so 'bout how to put dead people in the ground; the dead don't feel nothin'. But I keep my mouth shut 'n dig 'til I can't see outta the hole. Mr. Frank boosts me out 'n says he'll finish the job. I watch the dirt flyin' out 'til Mr. Frank's head barely shows when he stands up. He lays the shovel 'cross the hole, lifts 'imself out 'n sets on the dirt pile to rest.

"That's mighty deep," I say.

"Six feet; standard for military personnel."

"Mmmm, I saw some bluecoats buryin' somebody in a grave not near that deep t'other day."

"Where?" Mr. Frank jerks 'is head 'round 'n stares like I said the wrong thing.

"By the woods, past the buryin' trenches. The guard shooed me on down the road, but I hid in the brush 'n watched. Did I do somethin' bad?"

Mr. Frank laughs. "No Joe, not bad at all. You saw them bury me."

I jump back, nearly fallin' in the hole. "You ain't dead...are you?"

"No, but the guards thought I'd died from smallpox so they were afraid to touch me. They ordered my *shebang* mates to bury me away from the trenches. When night came, I dug out of the shallow grave, covered it up, and followed Stockade Creek to this place. That's why nobody came looking for me. I'm officially dead."

"Do you still have the pox?"

"Never did. I covered my face and arms with spots of blood to look like pox sores. I washed them off in the creek with your soap."

"You had me thinkin' you were a ghost."

"I didn't mean to deceive you my *niji*. I couldn't explain because my mates were planning to escape the same way. Now it won't matter since the cavalry's headed to Camp Sumter."

"Another reason I thought you might be a ghost, Tater didn't bark at you. He just went on point like you were a bird."

"That's easy to explain, but hard to understand, Joe. We'll talk more about it later. Now, we have a job to finish." He lifts the body from the cart, lowers it feet first in the grave 'n lets it fall to the bottom with the fence rail still tied on. We fill the grave with dirt 'n pack it down with the shovels.

"When the water goes down, Joe, bring some rocks to cover the grave. Now, I believe your mother asked you to say a prayer."

"I ain't much for prayin' out loud."

Mr. Frank nods like he understands. Liftin' 'is arms high, he talks with a voice like I ain't never heard; loud and hollow. "O Great Mystery, this man's spirit returns to the lodge of his ancestors before he received all the wisdom offered by Mother Earth. May his *mishomis* welcome him with open arms."

He lowers 'is arms 'n walks back to the cart. "Now, let's go burn this hay to throw off the bloodhounds if they come sniffing around the barn."

We pile the hay in the cart 'n I lead Ben back up the trail. About halfway to the barn, Mr. Frank stops, shades 'is eyes from the sun, 'n watches a bird flyin' towards us. "It's a red tail hawk," I say, "huntin' a field mouse."

"Brother to the eagle," Mr. Frank says. The hawk circles overhead 'n screeches at us. Mr. Frank whistles to the hawk. It hovers 'n then flies off towards the creek.

"I must stay here, Joe. Take the donkey to the barn but leave the cart here." He ain't makin' sense 'gain. While I unhitch Ben Mr. Frank piles the hay on the ground like he's gonna burn it out here in the open.

"Mr. Frank, we got a pit by the barn for burnin' trash."

"The hawk warns of danger, so I need to hide behind the hay for now. Put the donkey in the stall 'n go about your business. Come back here when all is well." A horse whinnies from the cabin, Ben answers 'n Tater starts barkin'. Must be tellin' us Momma's got comp'ny.

"Let's go Ben, 'fore somebody comes a lookin' for us." I take Ben to the barn 'n put 'im in 'is stall. Peepin' through the door crack, I see our neighbor on 'is horse talkin' to Momma. I can't hear what he's sayin' 'til he starts to leave.

"Y'all git over to the Camp 'fore it's too late, y' heah!" he hollers as he turns the horse 'round 'n slops through the mud towards the main road.

When the horse turns on to the main road, I run to the cabin. "Momma, what'd he say? Are the Yankees comin' now?"

She answers my question with mo' questions. "Where's Mr. Frank? Did he come back with you?"

"A red tail tol' 'im somebody's at the cabin, so he hid in the pasture."

She jerks 'er head back. "A talkin' hawk? That sun done worked on yo' head, chile. Go fetch 'im. I got news from the camp. Now hurry on."

Mr. Frank's hankerin' to hear Momma's news so we leave the cart 'n hay in the pasture. She meets us in the barn. "That storm flooded the stockade knockin' down a piece o' the wall 'n some prisoners got loose. Capt'n Wirtz says it's too many to track down, so he sent word for us to be on the lookout. What we gonna do now?"

"Wait for the Union cavalry to set the rest of the prisoners free."

"The camp's short o' vittles, so we gotta load the wagon 'n go tradin' with Mr. Dukes tomorrow mornin'. Joe, I reckon we better gather corn and sweet potatoes 'fore dark. We'll head for camp at first light, do our b'iness, 'n then come back 'fore the shootin' starts."

"Yessum." Thinkin' 'bout gittin' caught in the middle o' fightin' sets my heart on fire. That'll be somethin'—if I don't get killed jist watchin'. Mr. Frank gits the cart 'n takes care o' burnin' the spoilt hay. By sundown Momma 'n me done picked ten bushels o' corn 'n filled the wagon half full o' yams.

"That's the last o' the crops for tradin'," she says, "Reckon Massa Carter's gonna want somethin' he can plant next spring, bless his heart." We left two rows o' seed corn 'n some sweet potatoes in the field.

Momma tells Mr. Frank, "Make yo'self to home in the hayloft while I fix supper." I follow Momma to the kitchen, fetch the lantern, 'n go back to milk the cows 'n feed the mules 'n chickens.

I settle down to milkin' while Mr. Frank watches. My mind's full o' questions for the injun, startin' with one he still ain't answered yet. "What's yo' boy's name, the one 'bout my age?"

"I gave him my name, François, but he's not received his Ojibwe spirit name yet. We call him 'Little Frank' for now."

"You mean he ain't got all 'is names yet?"

"It's a little more involved than that. He'll get his other name when I return, and he'll go on a vision quest."

"A what?"

"A vision quest. All Ojibwe children must go on a vision quest. When I return to Odanah, I'll build him a small shelter near the shore of *Kitchi Gami,* the great lake. He'll stay there alone and without food, to commune with the *Manitos,* spirits that live with the Great Creator."

"Commune?"

That means the *Manitos* will talk to him through special dreams. They'll talk about why the Great Creator has given life to my son, and continues to sustain his life on this earth, and how he should live in balance with Mother Earth and all living creatures. And special knowledge may be given to my son in these dreams. The dreams may also reveal the name given to him by the spirits, even before he was born. This name is sacred, and is the most important of all his names. When he is ready, Little Frank will return to my lodge and seek the wisdom of an elder who will help interpret the dreams—and this will guide him through manhood, the third hill of life. Then it will be time to celebrate with a big feast, dancing, and singing."

"Oh," I say, my mind not takin' in everythin' he says. I set the half-full milk bucket down 'n take my stool to the other stall. "Mr. Frank, what dreams did you have on your vision quest—'n how did you get the name *Eagle-with-Three-Tongues?"*

"Visions and dreams are sacred trusts among fathers, sons and grandfathers. I can't tell you mine. But, I can tell you something about my name." I stop milkin' to listen. "My family belongs to the bird clan. To be named for the Eagle is a high honor. I learned four tongues: French from my father, Ojibwe from my mother, English from traders and Latin from Priests."

"But your name says three tongues, not four!"

"Yes, I turned away from Latin for a good reason. At the school I was sent to, the Jesuit priests allowed us to speak only French or English and read only Latin. Whenever I slipped and said something in Ojibwe, the priest would take a cane to my hide and make me sit on a fence rail the rest of the day. So, one day I ran away from the men of the waving stick, and returned to my family's wigiwam. I didn't have to go back to school because I am *métis*. Since then, I refuse to honor the Latin of the Black Robes because they do not honor children."

"Did you learn to read words writ down?"

"Yes, but learning is more than reading words. We can learn much from Mother Earth and the animals of the forests, birds that fly, fish that swim in the waters, the snakes, the insects—all have lessons they can share with men who claim them as brothers."

"Like that red tail hawk?"

"And like your dog, Tater."

"Oh yeah, Tater tells me lots; when he trees a possum or strikes a rabbit's trail or sees a stranger…but, why didn't he bark that day he found you?"

"Making noise is not the only way animals signal us. Remember what Tater did when he spotted me in the woods?"

I scratch my head tryin' to think. "He went on point. Why'd he do that 'stead o' barkin' like he's s'posed to?"

"He has bird dog blood that tells him not to bark, because it'll scare birds away."

"But, Mr. Frank, you ain't a bird…are you?"

He laughs 'n turns away. "Better you finish milking, Joe. I need the light to make my nest in the loft."

I don't like the way Mr. Frank plays with my mind. First, he says he's dead, then alive. He's both injun 'n white, but the white part ain't nothin' like white men I know—'cept Massa Carter. He talks with spirits usin' words I never heard. He thinks he's a bird 'n Tater does too, but that's a man I see scalin' the ladder to the loft. Nothin' 'bout *Eagle-With-Three-Tongues* makes sense, but that's all right, 'cause I feel like nothin' bad's gonna happen to me 'n Momma long as he's close by.

Totin' the milk back to the springhouse, I wonder…Will Mr. Frank show me how to find a better name than "Goober" to go with Joe?

11

Momma works 'til the moon comes up; churnin' milk, moldin' butter, 'n fryin' taters t'eat on the road to Camp Sumter in the mornin'. Too weary to wait up, I plop down on my pallet. The moon fills the cabin with soft light 'n the next thing I know Momma's hollerin' at me 'n the sun ain't up yet.

"Get outta bed, Joe. We got lots to do." She must o' stayed up all night gittin' ready. "Take Mr. Frank some breakfast 'n hitch up the mules."

"Yessum." I rub sleep from my eyes 'n slip on my overalls. Ol' red rooster crows like he's laughin' at me for gittin' up 'fore he did. Momma hands me a plate piled high with eggs, fatback, 'n biscuits. Then she pours hot coffee in a jar 'n wraps it with a dishrag.

"Don't climb the ladder with this hot coffee—might scald yo'self."

"Yessum." I smell the vittles on my way to the barn 'n my stomach growls like a dog. Mr. Frank's already down from the loft, splashin' water from the horse trough in 'is face.

"Morning, Joe. Something smells good."

"Here, Momma's fixed eggs 'n fatback for you...but don't birds eat jist worms?"

He flips water in my face 'n laughs. "Did you ever see an eagle scratching worms from the earth?" He takes the vittles 'n coffee 'n sets on Ben's cart to eat.

"No sir...I mean, *niji*, eagles 'round here hunt rabbits 'n squirrels mostly, sometimes chickens."

"Mmmm," Mr. Frank says with a mouth full o' eggs, "nothing but the best for the noblest of our flying brothers."

I've had more o' 'is spirit talk than I can tolerate. "Reckon I'd better hitch the mules 'n get ready to go sell peanuts at the camp." Mr. Frank finishes 'is coffee 'n helps me untangle the harnesses. When the wagon's ready Momma comes out totin' a basket o' vittles. I set the basket under the seat 'n give 'er a hand up.

"Where you figger on stayin' while we gone?" she asks Mr. Frank in a way that shows she ain't gonna like 'is answer.

He gits 'er message 'n shakes 'is head. "Where do you think I should wait for the Union soldiers?" This man reads folk good as he reads animals.

"Just so you know, every time we go tradin' with the sutler, somebody sneaks in the barn 'n steals eggs; camp guards I reckon, but I ain't sure."

"Then I won't be in the barn when the egg raiders come. They won't see me, but I'll see them."

Momma shrugs 'er shoulders. "I don't care 'bout knowin' who's stealin' eggs. Guards go hungry jist like prisoners do. Ain't nothin' I can do 'bout it nohow. Git Tater's rope 'n put 'im in the wagon, Joe." Mr. Frank lifts Tater up to the wagon. I jump down to fetch his tie-rope 'n climb back aboard. Momma flips 'er hand towards the mules. "Let's git, we wastin' time."

I untie the reins 'n cluck my tongue at the mules. As we move out, Mr. Frank hollers, "Thank you for the breakfast, Mrs. Della." Momma grins but he can't see 'er face.

She's still grinnin' when we make the turn on the main road where the big rain turned the dirt to red slop. The mules don't like floppin' through the mess, so I pop leather on their rumps to keep 'em movin'. Halfway to the camp, where the creek bends, the water washed out part o' the road.

"The creek's done swallowed up some o' the road, Momma."

"The Lord's will, chile. Hope the creek ain't too deep to cross at the camp." Momma turns to stare at the rushin' water. Then she hollers like she's snake bit, scarin' me plum silly.

"What's the matter, Momma?" She points to the creek. I holler "whoa," look back 'n see somethin' caught in a scrub oak hangin' over the water. Momma climbs down to look closer.

"I can't reach it, Joe, come hold my hand," she hollers. I tie the reins to the brake handle 'n jump off the wagon.

"It looks like a hat." Momma gives me 'er hand as she stretches over to pull the hat loose. The crossed swords on top gleam in the sun.

"Reckon 'tis," she says.

"What we gonna do with it?"

Momma looks 'round to make sure nobody's comin' up the road. She walks back to the wagon starin' at the hat. I climb on the wagon 'n then help 'er up. She settles on the seat board 'n presses the cavalry hat flat. "Hand me the vittles." I put the basket o' fried yams 'tween us. She dumps the cold yams outta the dishtowel into 'er lap, then rolls the hat up in the dishtowel 'n lays it in the bottom o' the basket. "Mr. Frank oughta know what to do with this hat," she says. "Now help me eat the rest o' these yams."

The wagon bumps over the railroad tracks into the spooky woods. I pop the reins but the mules won't go any faster in the mud.

"Let up on the po' critters, Joe."

"Yessum." She don't know how fast my heart's a poundin' 'gainst my overalls bib. The mules poke 'long the road through the woods 'n I look for bluecoats hidin' 'hind every tree. We finally get outta the woods—I can breathe again. We see wagons bunched up on the creek bank.

One o' Mr. Dukes' guards comes over 'n asks Momma. "You got goods to trade?" Momma nods to 'im. "Creek's up too high for wagons to cross. We'll walk your goods 'cross the creek to the store soon's we unload these other folks' wagons."

Momma gives me the last fried yam 'n mumbles, "Don't like this hidee-do, don't like it a'tall."

I fasten the reins so I can stand up to see what's goin' on. The black prisoners that usually gather wood are unloadin' the wagons. They set the goods on their heads 'n wade through the rushin' water holdin' a rope with one hand. Two men on t'other side pull the rope towards 'em as two on this side hold it steady. Every time a' empty wagon pulls out, I drive the mules closer to the creek. A soppin' wet prisoner leans against a back wheel.

Momma asks, "Where y'all from?"

"My name is Benjamin Carpenter of New York. Know where that is?"

"Reckon I do. You fightin' fo' the Yankees?"

He laughs, "Not since the rebs captured my whole regiment. Are you a slave, Miss…?"

Momma fakes bein' shy 'n don't answer. I ask the prisoner, "Do you know 'bout the Yankee soldiers a comin'?"

He laughs again shakin' his head. "You heard about that raiding party to the west?" I nod my head 'n lean closer to hear what he knows. "They have no reason to attack Camp Sumter. They've already cut the camp's supply lines. Besides, what's a handful of cavalry going to do with thousands of starving prisoners like us?"

I plop down on the wagon seat. "You mean they ain't comin'?"

Momma whines, "Lordy, Lordy, what we gonna do now?"

Another prisoner comes to help unload our wagon. "Wait!" Momma says. She climbs off the wagon 'n talks to Mr. Dukes' guard. He shakes 'is head 'n Momma starts wavin' 'er arms, like she's all stirred up. Then the guard motions to the prisoners to unload our wagon.

"We need some sacks or baskets for these sweet potatoes," the man called Benjamin hollers with a clear, sharp voice, not like field hands. I never heard a black man talk so fine. The guard comes over to inspect the load, with Momma at 'is heels, still fussin'.

"Take the corn on over 'n bring the sacks back for the potatoes," the guard orders the bluecoat prisoners.

"I tol' you, I wanna talk with Mr. Dukes 'fore y'all take my goods," Momma declares.

"Like I said, Della, Mr. Dukes is busy. He'll write down everything you brought. When the water goes down, y'all come back and settle up."

Momma huffs 'n folds 'er arms. "What we gonna do 'til then? What if the Yankee army gits here first?" She slaps 'er hand over 'er mouth like she didn't mean to say nothin' 'bout Yankees a comin'.

The guard laughs 'n straightens his back. "Your Yankee friends've turned tail and run back north where they come from." He waves 'is arm towards the prisoners. "Now, you boys get this wagon unloaded before I forget my Christian upbringing."

The guard goes back to the creek with Momma at 'is heels. The prisoners start unloadin' our corn. I try to ask 'bout the Yankee cavalry, but they keep on workin' like they don't heah me. I stretch out on the wagon seat, wonderin' what I'll tell Mr. Frank. Seems like this war's gonna go on 'n on 'n on.

The prisoners haul off the corn 'n come back with empty sacks for the sweet potatoes. "Y'all use some help?" I ask.

The man from New York jerks 'is head 'round 'n raises 'is eyebrows. "I don't want to make trouble for you, son. That slave woman might tell your folks."

I scratch my head. "Huh?"

"White children in the camp get whippings for just talking to prisoners like me. I'm surprised your folks sent you out alone with a slave."

"Mr. Benjamin, that's my momma over by the creek." He drops the sack. "She ain't gonna be a slave when Massa Carter comes…" I stop myself from sayin' too much 'n gettin' riled up.

The prisoner looks at me 'n turns to 'is helper. "Didn't I tell you things like this went on in the South?" They fill the sacks 'n go off to the creek whisperin' 'n lookin' back at me.

Momma's a mite sullen ridin' the wagon back to the farm. No sense tellin' 'er what the New York prisoner said; she'll git all riled up again. We come to the creek 'side the road where she found the hat.

"Lordy, Joe!" she hollers, just like 'fore 'n looks under the seat. "Where'd you put the dinner basket?"

"Whoa mules. I didn't put it nowhere, Momma. We left it in the wagon."

"I don't see it nowhere. That prisoner must o' took it. Did you see 'im take it, Joe?"

"No'm. Why'd he want yo' basket?"

"Maybe he thought it was vittles, but all it had was…Lordy, Lordy!" Momma bends over 'n moans. "Ohhh…what if he done found the hat 'n showed it to the guard?"

"We got trouble, Momma?"

Momma straightens up, folds 'er hands in 'er lap 'n closes 'er eyes. I wait 'til she's done prayin' 'fore startin' the mules. In a minute, she opens 'er eyes 'n changes 'er tune.

"Don't matter now. What's done's done. It's in the Lord's hands. Git up mules 'n take us to the farm." I slap the reins to git us movin'. We pull in the yard while the sun's still high 'n dryin' up the mud.

"Look a'there," Momma says, pointin' to a double set o' boot tracks 'cross the yard, "two comin' 'n two goin'. Some folk gonna be eatin' eggs fo' supper."

"Wonder if Mr. Frank saw who done it?" I talk real loud so he'll know it's us, but only Ben 'n the chickens answer me. Momma climbs off the wagon without help 'n goes straight to the cabin. I turn Tater loose 'n unhitch the mules, lookin' over my shoulder for Mr. Frank the whole time. He's gotta know 'bout the cavalry ain't comin'.

"Mr. Frank?" I call, 'n then stop to listen. No answer. "Find that bird man, Tater." Tater runs 'round sniffin' every stall. I climb to the loft like I'm fetchin' peanuts to roast. He ain't there either. I throw some bunches o' peanuts down 'n leave 'em to fix later. Firewood's still too wet to cook goobers today.

Satisfied that Mr. Frank ain't in the barn, I wander over to the cabin to see if Momma has any scraps fo' Tater. Momma's at the kitchen table with 'er head layin' on 'er arms. She hears me comin' 'n wipes 'er eyes with the apron.

"You got any scraps for Tater?" I ask, makin' like I don't see she been cryin'. She drums 'er fingers on the table.

"Set a spell, Joe," she says with trouble coverin' her face. I set 'cross the table from 'er 'n smile, hopin' nothin's wrong. "We done come on hard times, chile. Looks like the Lord's done got too busy helpin' other folk mo' fittin' fo' His grace." Tears roll down 'er cheeks. I drop my eyes 'n stare at the table. "Folk at the camp say Massa Carter ain't comin' back to the farm. He done lost both 'is legs 'n can't run this place no mo'. With Massa Carter gone, I figure Mr. Dukes ain't got no reason to make good on our trade today. I don't know how much longer we gonna hold out." She gits up 'n paces back 'n forth huggin' herself. "We'd be fools t'eat the seed corn 'n taters."

"But Momma, we got peas 'n beans in the garden, 'n a loft full o' peanuts." I try to break 'er sad spell. "Me 'n Tater can catch rabbits. We got lots o' chickens."

She comes over 'n pulls my head close. "I know, but when folk hear 'bout Massa Carter…I don't know…"

"What you sayin', Momma?"

"I don't want you worryin' none, Joe, jist keep yo' head 'n hope this war's gonna soon be over. Nobody knows what trouble rides the wind, ain't nobody a coming to help us."

"Mr. Frank…"

Momma turns me loose. "Uh uh, chile, don't see 'im 'round here, do you? I figgered he'd take off first chance he got 'n head north to freedom. No sir, Mr. Joe, you the only man in this house,

the only hope yo' momma's got. Now I reckon you better go to
the big house 'n find some more shotgun shells. We gonna need
'em when trouble knocks on our door."

"Yessum." I swallow the lump in my throat. Looks like the
war's gonna come to our place right soon 'n I'm the only soldier
on duty. I stop on the front porch to look 'round once more for any
signs that *Eagle-With-Three-Tongues* ain't took t' wing 'n flied
'way. Then I head to the big house 'n fetch all the shotgun shells I
can tote without blowin' a hole in my belly.

12

Momma sleeps tight with the loaded shotgun by 'er bed, but I'm too uneasy to close my eyes. I git up to let Tater in. Momma hears the door creak, jolts straight up in bed, 'n reaches for the shotgun. She sees me in the moonlight.

"Where you goin'?"

"Lettin' Tater in to sleep with me." Momma's actin' more jumpy'n ever b'fore. She's right scary.

"Leave 'im out," she says 'n rolls over like she ain't gonna take no sass from me. I latch the door 'n stand by the window lookin' at the moon.

"Fly back to yo' nest in the loft, Mr. Frank," I whisper over 'n over 'til heavy eyes draw me back to my pallet.

Next mornin' Momma's mood ain't changed—she don't sing fixin' breakfast. She don't talk much while we eat 'cept to tell me to gather eggs 'n let the cows 'n mules out to pasture.

"Plenty eggs today," I sing out from the porch after robbin' the hen's nests. Momma comes out to git the basket with a little smile like she's found some hope in that big basket o' eggs.

"Joe, I want you to go see how far the creek water went down last night."

"Yessum."

"If it's down far 'nough to cross, I wanna go see Mr. Dukes soon's the sun gits high."

I take off for the creek with Momma's words driftin' in the wind. Tater runs to the cornfield, I take the dry pasture trail. A red tail hawk swoops down 'head o' me 'n grabs a field mouse. I whistle like Mr. Frank, but I reckon the hawk's too busy catchin' breakfast to answer. It flies off in the woods to finish eatin'.

As I scoot 'tween the fence rails, I see Corporal Tolliver's grave 'n 'member I gotta cover it with rocks. I move over to the rise to see if the water's gone down. The rust colored water's dropped a lot but it's still too deep 'n swift to pick up rocks. I don't like bein' down here by myself with Corporal Tolliver nohow. What if the Lord don't let 'im in the pearly gates? His ghost might take a notion to rattle my gourd on the way down to the fiery furnace.

"Come on, Tater, let's get outta this graveyard." Tater stops to drink from a water hole right where Momma 'n me buried the bluecoat cavalryman. "Git, Tater, git back from that death pit." I run down the creek a ways to make Tater chase me, hopin' the bluecoat's body ain't stuck in the blackberry vines. If the body's in the creek, buzzards oughta be circlin' by now. I look up but don't see nothin' 'cept crows flyin' 'round the trees. Reckon they're fussin' at a hawk or owl messin' with their nests. Maybe Mr. Frank's hidin' out 'round the creek 'n wants me to find 'im.

"Tater, go git 'im," I holler. But Tater don't track up 'n down the creek, he heads for the open pasture 'n circles 'round a stand o' broom straw. He slows down 'n sniffs 'long the ground. He stops 'n points.

"Mr. Frank, *niji*, it's me, Joe." The crows git quiet. I wait. "Mr. Frank?" No answer.

I walk slow towards the broom straw 'til Tater's right at my feet, still on point. A stick cracks under my foot sendin' a covey o' quail flutterin' outta the brush. My skin draws tight all over. This time Tater flushes real birds, not a man who's claimin' to be one. Sapped outta hope, I call Tater 'n start back to the cabin.

"No use lookin' for somebody who's gone for good, ol' dog, no use a'tall."

When I tell Momma the creek's down, she puts me to work.
"Clean out the milkin' stalls 'n split some stove wood," she says.

"Yessum." It's the hardest work a boy can do 'round here.
After shovelin' manure, I split stove wood 'til I'm plumb give out.
I lean the ax 'gainst the chinaberry tree b'hind the cabin 'n sprawl
on the washstand under a shade tree.

Momma sees me restin' 'n hollers, "Fetch some milk from
the springhouse 'n I'll fix us somethin' t'eat." I'm more tired than
hungry, but I roll off my restin' place. Inside the springhouse I
take long breaths o' cool damp air. I wanna stay here a spell, but
Momma's a waitin'. As I lean over to get the bucket o' milk,
somethin' taps on the back wall.

"Tater?" Naw, can't be Tater 'cause he's sleepin' on the
front porch. Tap, tap, tap, again. I peek through the narrow cracks
'tween the boards, but ain't nothin' movin'. Tap, tap, tap. I go
outside to look, but ain't nothin' 'cept leaves 'n vines on the path
to the creek.

"Somebody there?" Leaves rustle 'bove my head. A stick as
long's my arm falls 'cross the trail smack in front o' me. I jump
back thinkin' it's a snake. It's got feathers stuck in a slit at one
end. I look up—it's Mr. Frank, straddlin' a big poplar limb.

"Don't be scared, Joe."

"Mr. Frank!"

He swings down from the tree 'n picks up the stick with the
feathers on it. I'm shakin' all over. "A gift from brother hawk,"
he says, strokin' the long feathers.

"What...where...?"

"Not now, Joe. Run tell your mother I need to talk to her." I
take off to the cabin fast as I can run. Momma starts to fuss at me
for not bringin' in the milk.

"But Momma, Mr. Frank's back!" She hurries out to the
back stoop to see for 'erself. Mr. Frank shows 'is face from b'hind
the springhouse.

"Lordy, Lordy, Joe, go look down the road 'n see if
anybody's a comin'." I race through the cabin to the front yard 'n

back. Momma waves Mr. Frank to the cabin. "I'm proud to see you, Mr. Frank. Lordy, I could jist hug yo' neck."

"A piece of cornbread will do fine," he laughs. "A man gets hungry sitting in a tree all morning." Momma sends me to the springhouse for the milk I forgot. When I git back she's tellin' Mr. Frank what she heard at Camp Sumter the day b'fore.

"We got word the Yankee soldiers ain't comin'. Them bluecoat raiders set fire to a train haulin' vittles to the camp 'n turned north. Reckon why they did that?"

Mr. Frank shakes 'is head. "Nothing about this war makes any sense." He nearly chokes on a bite o' cold cornbread. Momma takes the cornbread 'n crumbles it in 'is jar o' sweetmilk.

"There, goes down better this way," she says, handin' 'im a spoon. He sips a bit o' milk first.

"This is not buttermilk?" Momma shakes 'er head 'n smiles. "I like it," he says.

"We figgered you ran off to catch up with yo' bluecoat folk."

"I wouldn't know where to look for them. I was hoping they'd raid the camp and turn the prisoners loose so I'd have company traveling north. Looks as though I'll have to find my way home alone. I hope to make it in time for ricing." He finishes eatin' 'n I see sadness fall over 'is face. "Yesterday, while you were gone, I searched the creek for the cavalryman's body, but didn't have any luck. It must've washed on down to the stockade, but I don't think he can be traced back to this place."

"Momma found 'is hat."

"His hat? Where?"

"In the creek where it runs by Oglethorpe road," Momma says, "I reckon it's his."

"What did you do with it?"

"Wrapped it in a cloth 'n hid it in our vittles basket."

"But somebody took the basket when Momma turned 'er back, I 'spect it was the prisoners that unloaded the wagon."

Momma cuts 'er eyes at me 'n shakes 'er head. "We ain't sho', but I'm gonna be in a heap o' trouble if the wrong folk find that hat in my basket."

"I wouldn't worry, Mrs. Della, it's not treason to find a hat on the road. You just go about your business as usual. If a prisoner took your basket, it's likely he'll keep the hat to trade for tobacco. If a guard finds it, he'll trade it too."

"I hope you right. But it won't take much for Capt'n Wirtz to put me to work at the camp with the other house women 'n field hands."

"You mean the slaves?"

"Yessuh, but 'fore he left fo' the war, Massa Carter done promised he gonna set me free."

It's the first time Momma talks 'bout her'n Massa Carter's bi'ness in front o' me. It starts me wonderin' 'bout the Yankee prisoner makin' fun o' my white skin; 'bout am I slave or free? Momma don't tolerate my wonderin'. She turns to stone every time I ask somethin' 'bout who I am. If only Mr. Frank would ask 'er in front o' me. 'Fore I take 'nother breath, my wish comes true.

"Mrs. Della, could I ask you a question about Joe?"

Momma's eyes get wide like a possum caught up a gum tree with no way down. "I reckon," she mumbles.

"Does Joe belong to Mr. Carter? Is he a slave?"

Momma bites 'er lip 'n hugs 'erself. She gits up from the table like she's gonna clear off the dishes. "My boy ain't no slave, ain't never been one. And that's all I gotta say 'bout that."

Mr. Frank sees Momma's fixin' to cry. He pushes back from the table 'n starts talkin' 'bout somethin' else. "If you don't mind, I'll wait until after sundown to leave. I wonder if I could trouble you for a grubstake so I won't starve on the way to Wisconsin." When he talks 'bout leavin', Momma breaks down 'n cries.

"Lordy, Lordy, Mr. Frank, when I git back, I'll fix you 'nough to eat for a week." She dabs 'er wet eyes with 'er apron. "Joe, hitch up the wagon. We gotta go git our trade goods."

"Yessum."

Mr. Frank says he'll hide in the barn loft 'til we get back. On the way to the camp the sun beats down on us like a ball 'o fire. We come to the creek, where some paroled prisoners are tryin' to build a log crossin', but the heavy timbers keep floatin' down the creek. The guard in charge motions for me to drive the mules 'round the workers. The mules git to the edge o' the swift water, but won't move on through. The prisoner from New York notices our stubborn team.

"You folks need help?" he hollers. Then he walks over, takes hold o' the harness 'n leads the mules through waist-deep water to the other side.

"Much obliged to you," Momma says as he starts back to 'is work.

He tips 'is hat 'n says, "Madam, I'm only returning the favor." He tips 'is hat again, but this time he holds it high in the air like he's showin' it off.

"Lordy," Momma gasps.

"What's the matter?" I ask.

"Nothin', nothin', jist go on to the store."

We go straight to Mr. Dukes' store. I help Momma off the wagon, then lead the mules over to a waterin' trough to wait. Some folk come by wantin' peanuts. I tell 'em I'll be back tomorrow with a sack full.

Momma storms outta the store stompin' 'cross the porch 'n down the steps totin' her missin' basket.

Mr. Dukes runs after 'er hollerin', "Now don't you go running off mad like that. There's a war going on."

She climbs on the wagon 'n barks at me, "Let's go."

'Fore I can untie the reins, Mr. Dukes takes a hold o' the mule's harness, "Y'all ain't going nowhere 'til my men saddle up." Momma bites 'er lip 'n stares straight 'head, refusin' to look at the sutler. I set bakin' in the sun feelin' Momma's 'bout to bust.

Two guards trot their horses from back o' the store 'n pull up to our wagon. Mr. Dukes turns the reins loose 'n orders 'em, "You men escort this woman to the Carter Plantation and help her load all the provisions y'all can find. Look in the barn, the corncrib and the fields. Haul the goods back here, and make more'n one trip if need be."

Momma speaks up, "What we gonna eat?"

"Like I tol' you, I got thirty thousand mouths to feed over here and you got just two. While these men load the wagon, you'n Goober Joe put a little aside for your selves. And you can go up to Oglethorpe and buy what you need with the money I give you."

Mr. Dukes never called me "Goober" b'fore. He's actin' different, like the war done got in 'is craw. Momma waves 'er hand towards the mules. I turn 'em 'round in the road 'n head back to the creek. "Money, hmmph," Momma grunts, "them Confed dollars ain't worth nothin'."

On the way back to the farm Momma starts moanin'. "What we gonna do, chile, what we gonna do?"

"Don't worry, Momma, we'll git by. We got milk 'n eggs 'n apples 'n rabbits 'n…"

"It's what we got in the barn loft that worries me," she says under 'er breath.

"Oh, Mr.…." she clamps a hand over my mouth 'n looks up to see if the guards heah us talkin'. They pay us no mind. I gotta to figger a way to warn Mr. Frank 'fore we get there. I search the sky for a hawk to carry a message, but I ain't learned bird talk yet. We left Tater in the barn with Mr. Frank. I gotta act fast.

"Whoa mules." I stop the wagon at the trail to the big house 'n hand the reins to Momma. "I'm gonna run to the barn to warn Mr. Frank we got company," I whisper. The guards stop 'n turn 'round.

"What you stopping for?" a guard asks.

"I gotta run tie up my dog so he don't spook yo' horses."

"I've seen your dog. He ain't no bother," said the older guard. He's the same man who came to the farm with Corporal Tolliver 'n Mr. Turner last week. 'Fore I can jump down from the wagon, the guard takes off to the barn. The other guard waves us to follow 'long. Momma hands me the reins 'n starts moanin' again.

"Lordy, Lordy, deliver Mr. Frank from 'is enemies, amen." I whistle loud as I can like I'm callin' my dog, hopin' Mr. Frank hears my signal in time to run away.

13

Momma jumps off the wagon 'fore it stops movin' 'n runs to the cabin. I don't know what she's up to, so I jist stop the mules in the middle o' the yard 'n wait. The guard that rode ahead is already lookin' over the corn he's got to pick. The other guard ties up 'is horse 'n heads to the barn. I whistle for Tater—to warn Mr. Frank, but Tater don't come out. It's strange Ben ain't brayin' at me when I whistle.

Momma hollers, "Joe, come're 'n help me."

I wrap the reins 'round the brake stob 'n hurry inside. Momma sets on the bed with 'er quilt layin' 'cross 'er lap. "What's wrapped in yo' quilt?" I ask.

She pulls back a corner to show the stock o' the shotgun. "I ain't gonna let 'em take Mr. Frank back to die in that stockade."

"Momma! You gonna git shot 'n killed."

"They ain't totin' guns. Go out 'n watch. Don't help 'em 'n don't talk to 'em. Jist act dumb when they talk to you."

"But, Momma…"

"Do like I tol' you, chile. I'll be watchin' from the window."

"Yessum."

I go out 'n mess 'round the wagon, actin' like I'm busy. They start pickin' our seed corn. One guard brings a' armload o' ears 'n dumps 'em in the wagon bed.

"Ain't y'all got no sacks?" he asks. I hunch my shoulders 'n walk b'hind the wagon. "Where you goin' boy? Come help us pick this corn." I keep on movin' like I ain't heard nothin' 'n head to the well to fetch water for the mules. The guard gives up 'n goes back to pickin' corn. I take my time totin' buckets o' water to the mules, mindin' my Momma. The guards fill the wagon bed with corn 'bout three ears deep. "We left y'all a dozen stalks for seed," the older guard says. "Now, where're the sweet potatoes, in the barn?" I act like I don't heah.

"Don't bother askin' that half-breed," the younger guard says. "He's dumber'n a rusty horseshoe nail." They go to the barn 'n I hold my breath.

"Hey, look what I found," the guard hollers. I look back to see if Momma's got the shotgun ready. She done moved to the door, standin' with 'er hand hid 'hind 'er back.

The guard waves my sacks over 'is head. "It's Croaker sacks, a whole bunch!" Mr. Frank ain't in the loft, or he's hidin' under the hay. Soon the two men tote sacks o' yams to the wagon 'n stack 'em on top o' the corn.

"We left yo' peanuts in the loft, Joe, ain't enough to fool with," the older guard winks at me. I hide a smile 'n tuck my head. He throws a' empty sack to me 'n says, "For that little favor, you gotta help us pick them peas 'n beans."

I follow 'em to the garden 'n glance over my shoulder at Momma standin' in the door. She shoos me on like I'm doin' the right thing. I pick real slow, leavin' more'n I take—we gotta eat too. The guards put the beans 'n peas in the wagon 'n head for the orchard. Most o' the apples're wormy, but I help 'em fill three sacks anyway.

"These worms'll give the cider a little more kick," a guard laughs. We haul the sacks to the wagon. I lean 'gainst the sideboards 'n take a deep breath. They didn't find Mr. Frank so Momma didn't hafta shoot nobody. But they ain't done. The older guard pulls the strings outta one empty sack 'n lays 'em over the side o' the wagon.

"I counted a dozen layin' hens and maybe fifteen fryers runnin' loose," he says. "We'll take all the fryers 'cept one and leave two or three hens." Momma's real proud of 'er chickens. She talks to 'em like they's 'er chillun. I look back to see if she's gonna try to save 'er flock. But she jist stands in the door a watchin', ain't movin' a muscle. She ain't gonna shoot nobody over stealin' chickens. The guards round up the chickens, drive 'em in the barn 'n shut the door. After a lot o' squawkin' they open the door to let two hens 'n the red rooster flutter out. They haul the chickens to the wagon with their feet tied 'n stuff 'em in croaker sacks.

"Maybe they'll make it to the camp alive if we leave now," the older guard says. "All right, who's gonna drive the team back to camp?" He hollers so Momma can heah from inside the cabin. She comes to the porch with 'er arms folded, leavin' the shotgun in the cabin. She stares at the wagon full o' goods 'n shakes 'er head. Somehow Mr. Frank hid 'imself good 'nough so a fight didn't break out in our yard today. Now I won't be diggin' two more graves.

The guards mount up 'n lead us in our loaded wagon down the road, with chickens squawkin'. Momma sets 'side me moanin' all the way to the camp. We pull up in front o' the store 'n Mr. Dukes comes out to look over the goods.

"Is that all y'all found?" The guards nod their heads 'n slide off their horses. "Well, Della, I figured y'all had a better crop than this."

Momma stands up in the wagon. "I'm wonderin' what Massa Carter's gonna say when he comes back to the farm 'n I tell 'im you took 'is seed corn 'n sweet potatoes."

Mr. Dukes laughs with his mouth drawn crooked. "You know Major Carter's in no shape to worry about planting crops. A man's got to have legs to work a plantation, especially with all the slaves run off...'cepting you, of course." He hollers to the guards, "Tie up yo' hosses and unload this wagon before the sun spoils everything." He goes in the store 'n comes back with a handful o' money. "Here you go, Della. Forty dollars oughta cover what I owe you."

Momma stares at the Confed dollars. "I can use a sack o' meal 'n some flour."

"Ain't got none to spare. Now you take this money and get gone before I change my mind and take some back." He grits 'is teeth 'n shoves the money at Momma. Bad times done turned the sutler real sour. Momma takes the forty dollars 'n moans. Mr. Dukes whips 'round 'n stomps back in the store.

"Let's git outta this devil's holdin' pen, Joe. It's startin' to smell worse'n ever."

I drive the empty wagon back to the creek. The paroled prisoners done quit workin' 'n they settin' on the ground. The man from New York sees us 'n offers to lead the mules back 'cross the high water. Momma straightens up 'n sheds 'er mad face when he speaks to 'er.

"May I be of service to you again, dear lady," he says touchin' 'is hat brim like b'fore.

Momma smiles 'n nods 'er head. He wades through the water pullin' the mules b'hind 'im. When we clear the stream on t'other side, he tells Momma, "I appreciate the gift you left in the basket." He touches the crossed swords on the front of 'is hat. "Next time, be more careful where you hide Union contraband."

Momma's mouth drops open. The man wades back into the creek 'n we head into the spooky woods. Momma says, "Lordy, we done been beat up 'n blessed all in the same day. Let's git to the farm 'fore the sun goes down."

We come outta the woods 'n cross the railroad track 'n I ask Momma, "Did Mr. Frank leave, or jist hide real good?"

"Lord only knows, chile. That man sho' is a mystery to me; it's like he's watchin' us from far off when we don't even know it."

"Sorta like a hawk?" I say. Momma nods 'er head a little, like she's humorin' me. I raise my hand to block out the settin' sun 'n search the sky for a sign from *Eagle-With-Three-Tongues* or from brother hawk. But only buzzards cut 'cross the sky, high 'bove the woods.

"Uh oh," I nearly choke, pointin' to the circlin' birds o' death. Momma lifts the brim o' 'er hat up to look.

"Lordy, I reckon them buzzards done found the cavalryman. Heaven help 'is po' ol' soul."

I can't push the mules no faster, so I decide it's a good time to talk serious to Momma. "What we gonna do if Massa Carter don't come back?" The wagon bumps on down the road a bit 'fore Momma answers.

"You gonna wear out yo' mind with worry, chile. The Lord looks after the birds, the beasts 'n the fishes. He'll sho'ly look after you 'n me."

"I jist wish we had a man to help the Lord with them chores."

She puts 'er arm 'round me. "Joe, you the only man we need."

"I reckon so, only..." I finally work up nerve 'nough to speak what's been on my mind a long time. "...only, I wish I had a daddy." Momma drops 'er arm from 'round my shoulders 'n buries 'er face in 'er hands. I knew I'd strike a nerve even 'fore I spoke, but somethin' inside me's churnin' like a wash pot boilin' over. I can't stop now.

"Momma, Corporal Tolliver used to say I'm Massa Carter's boy. And that prisoner from New York figgered I didn't b'long to you 'cause you brown 'n I'm white."

Momma raises 'er head 'n says, "Ain't I tol' you not to listen to what other folk say 'bout you?"

"Yessum, but you say I'm a man now. What kind o' man am I? You tol' Mr. Frank I ain't no slave, but other folk treat me like I am one. Am I slave or free? You're my momma, so tell me the truth." Momma nods 'er head, then shakes it from side to side, then nods 'gain.

"What I say don't matter, chile. That's what this war's all 'bout. One side says you free, t'other says you slave. But it's up to you 'n the Lord. You can be free as you wanna be."

She locks 'er dark eyes on mine, like she's seein' deep down inside me. Suddenly, I feel tall as a bear 'n small as a fox at the same time. I wanna soar like eagles 'n dart like hummingbirds.

"I reckon I need a vision quest."

"A what?"

"Oh, somethin' injun boys do to figger out what they 'sposed to do with the rest o' their lives. And, they git their real names."

"But you have a real name," Momma says. "I named you myself."

"Corporal Tolliver called me Goober, that ain't real. I mean I need a family name like all the white folk have 'n slave folk don't."

"Umm huh," Momma says, like she ain't sure I'm talkin' sense. The mules turn on the trail to the big house without me pullin' on the reins. Momma laughs when I nearly fall off the wagon 'cause I ain't mindin' the team. "If I had to give you 'nother name right now, I'd call you Joe Curious."

"Momma, jist 'llow me to find my own name."

"You ain't got time to worry 'bout namin' yo'self all over right now. We got jist 'nough daylight to do the milkin' 'n feed the..." she 'members the guards took 'er chickens, "...what chickens we got left."

When I go to put up the mules for the night, Ben's not in the stall. And the cart's gone. Then I 'member that Tater's been gone all day too. I whistle for Tater 'n rush out to the pasture searchin' for my missin' buddies.

"Tater, Ben, come on, boys. Heah, heah." No sign o' my donkey or my dog. Momma brings the milk buckets out to the barn. "Momma, Tater 'n Ben're gone, they don't answer me!" She shrugs 'er shoulders 'n hands me the buckets.

"They gonna be hungry soon 'n come draggin' in. Now git the milkin' done 'fore you lose daylight."

"My cart's gone, too! Somebody done stole it!"

Momma follows me to Ben's stall. She stops where I left the cart 'n looks 'round. "Them guards didn't take yo' cart. I reckon Mr. Frank did."

"No...no, Mr. Frank wouldn't steal nothin', he's a good man." Tears come to my eyes, but I bite my lip to keep from cryin'.

"War changes folk, Joe. I'll go to the cabin 'n see what else he done took. Now, milk the cows 'fore they bust." After talkin' like Mr. Frank's turned on us, Momma hangs 'er head low all the way to the cabin. I give the cows some hay to chew on while I milk 'em. I can't get Mr. Frank off my mind as I squirt the milk into the bucket. I wonder what part o' his blood made my *niji* steal from me—injun or Yankee?

14

Momma prays long 'n hard 'fore we go to bed. I hold still
listenin' 'cause that's the only way I can tell what's on 'er mind.

"Lord, you done heaped mo' blessin's on me than I deserve.
You know I'm much obliged, but I got sorrow heavy on my heart.
'Tain't yo' fault Lord, the Devil put it there when I strayed from
yo' ways. I'm askin' Lord, fill my heart with kindness. If you got
any left over, send it to that Yankee man 'n make 'im bring back
my boy's donkey 'n dog." She goes on to talk with the Lord 'bout
the war, the hot weather, 'er sore back, 'n Massa Carter. She puts
him in 'er prayers, but not Missy Carter 'n the girls. "And one mo'
thing, Lord, I'm blessed you done give me a fine son who's gonna
look after 'is Momma 'til kingdom come...Amen." Hearin'
Momma talk 'bout me to the Lord helps settle me down on my
pallet.

But sleep don't come easy tonight, too much on my mind.
Every time I drift off a bad dream wakes me up, mostly 'bout
bluecoats 'n rebels shootin' at each other 'cross the flooded creek.
Dead bodies're floatin' down the creek that's runnin' red with
blood. Momma's screamin' at me to get outta the way. But I can't
'til I find Tater 'n Ben.

No sooner'n I go back to sleep the dreams start up again. In
'nother dream Tater's barkin' 'n Ben's brayin', callin' for help but
my feet stick to the floor. I wake up in a sweat 'n pull my feet off
the pallet to run outside. But it's jist a dream. I git a' empty

feelin' inside like my buddies won't ever come back again—Ben, Tater…'n Mr. Frank. I roll back on the pallet 'n stare at the moonlight shinin' in the window 'til my weary mind pulls me back to my dreams.

At first light ol' red rooster crows but I ain't ready to git up. Momma acts like she don't hear 'im, jist layin' on 'er back with eyes wide open starin' up at the oak shingles.

"You feelin' sickly, Momma?" I ask. She rolls 'er head to let me know she ain't comin' down with somethin'. I stand up to stretch my legs 'n yawn. Somethin' outside answers my yawn with a whine 'n I heah tiny steps patter 'cross the porch. Sounds like a dog, but Tater's gone. I rush to the door 'n swing it open. Tater sets there waggin' 'is tail 'n showin' 'is teeth like he's grinnin' at me.

I holler, "Tater's back!" I kneel down to hug my dog 'n he licks my face all over.

Momma shakes off 'er low mood 'n comes to look out the door. "Lordy, my prayer done been answered. Praise the Lord! Reckon you might find yo' donkey's come back too. Run over to the barn 'n look…" Her voice drifts off 'cause I'm already racin' to Ben's stall.

I pull open the barn door 'n start hollerin'. "Momma, Momma, Ben's back, too 'n so's my cart!" Momma starts to come out, but 'members she's in her sleepin' gown. 'Spectin' Mr. Frank's watchin' close by, Momma goes back inside 'n comes out wearin' a housedress 'n tyin' 'er apron. I climb the ladder hopin' I'll find Mr. Frank settin' cross-legged on his nest o' hay.

"Mr. Frank? *Niji?*" Nothin' 'cept pigeons answer my call. "He ain't up here," I holler to Momma. I walk 'tween stacks o' hay bales 'n throw open the loft door to let the mornin' sun in so I can see better. Mr. Frank's nest's empty 'cept for a hick'ry stick. It's the one with feathers on it that he dropped on the trail 'hind the springhouse. I take it to the ladder hole 'n show it to Momma.

"Mr. Frank left his spirit stick."

Momma shakes 'er head, "Spirit stick, hmmph, it's jist a stick with feathers on it." She can't hide bein' sad 'bout Mr. Frank leavin' 'gain, maybe headin' north to help 'is boy harvest wild rice. As she walks back to the cabin, I run my fingers up 'n down the stick wonderin' why Mr. Frank left it. Maybe if I put it to my ear…naw, sticks can't talk…but this one's got a spirit. I close my eyes 'n listen real hard.

Nothin'.

I crawl down the ladder, hold the stick high in the air 'n turn 'round tryin' to see the barn with new eyes. Ben paws at 'is stall door breakin' the spell. "I know I got chores to do, Ben." I lay the stick in the cart 'n let the cows 'n mules out to pasture. Ben kicks 'is door again.

"I ain't forgot you, ol' buddy." I lift the latch 'n let 'im push open the gate. "I wish you could tell me where you'n Tater went." Ben waits for 'is mornin' scratch behind the ears 'n then he trots out the gate. My eyes fall to the ground followin' Ben's tracks 'tween ruts cut into the soft ground jist outside the barn door. I look out the other barn door. There ain't no ruts goin' that way. Is that the secret? Ben 'n the cart didn't go outside the pasture the whole time I missed 'em. Tater must o' been with 'im too…and Mr. Frank!

I close the gate 'n set my mind to followin' the cart tracks that might lead me to Mr. Frank. "Joe, O Joe," Momma hollers from the kitchen. "Come git somethin' t'eat. It's ready." No use tellin' Momma yet. First I'll eat, then I'll git Ben 'n Tater to help me track down Mr. Frank.

While I stuff my mouth with hoecakes 'n sorghum syrup, Momma jist picks at 'er vittles—she's got somethin' on 'er mind she ain't willin' to talk 'bout. She don't even tell me 'bout the work I gotta do today. That's all right with me. I'll get done 'fore she comes back to 'er right mind 'n sends me to chop wood or draw water or dig up the sweet potatoes the guards left.

I gotta find a reason to go to the creek, so I rush to the back stoop 'n pick up the seine.

"Me'n Tater gonna catch some perch or sunfish for supper," I holler 'n jump off the stoop 'fore Momma has time to say no.

I cut through the peanut patch to the pasture 'n follow the cart tracks. Ben brays 'n lopes over to join me'n Tater in the hunt. The tracks lead to the wagon trail. They ain't easy to see on hard ground, so I jist go 'long the trail 'side the fence.

"Ben I'm countin' on you to show me where Mr. Frank took y'all." Tater barks like he's bein' left out. "You too, Tater, you too."

We go all the way to the creek where we buried Corporal Tolliver. Tater runs over 'n sniffs at the rocks on the grave 'n...wait! I didn't put them rocks there. I climb over the fence to git closer. There ain't no fresh cart tracks, but somebody done made a trail from the creek to the grave. Must o' been Mr. Frank. He hauled rocks in 'is hands 'stead o' usin' the cart. I walk outside the fence a ways. Ben trots 'long 'head o' me inside the fence, then stops 'n nickers like a horse. Fresh cart tracks run under the fence rails.

"Ben, this's gotta be where Mr. Frank led you outta the pasture. Com'on, Tater. You stay here, Ben." He don't cotton to me leavin' 'im by hisself but, without no halter, I'm 'fraid he'll run off.

Me 'n Tater follow the tracks 'long the edge o' the cotton field. The seine slows me down so I lean it 'gainst the fence 'til we git back. Tater runs on to the end o' the field. He barks twice, then sets 'n waits for me. Why'd Tater stop? He ain't on point, jist settin' there lookin' at the creek. It's a pile o' creek rocks with fresh dirt scattered 'round jist like at Corporal Tolliver's grave. A grave! Who dug it? Who's in it? The cart tracks run on past the grave. I sho' need that spirit stick I left in the barn. Its power might help me figger out what Mr. Frank did here.

The tracks lead through a patch o' brush 'n over a little branch that flows to the creek. Fresh wheel ruts run outta the branch on t'other side 'n cut through the brush to the piney woods. The tracks git lost in the thick pine straw.

"Tater, show me where y'all took the cart." Tater circles 'round 'n 'round through the big pines like he's huntin' a rabbit. He ain't much help, so I mosey down towards the creek. I walk 'long the creek bank a ways, 'til I see the main road to Camp Sumter. I figger Mr. Frank wouldn't o' come this close to the road where guards might see 'im. Takin' a deep breath, I close my eyes hopin' for a sign from Mr. Frank.

"Mr. Frank, what next?" As I turn to go back, I see Tater ain't with me. I find 'im hunkered down back up the creek, whinin' 'n pawin' at brush marks in the sand. Looks like the same marks Mr. Frank made to cover where Momma 'n me dragged the cavalryman outta the creek. Followin' the brush marks to the woods, I find wheel marks from the cart cut in the dirt 'n a boot print that ain't brushed over.

"Good dog, Tater." Mr. Frank must o' found the cavalryman's body right here! He hauled the body 'way from the road so nobody could see 'im diggin' the grave. The buzzards circlin' 'round—they led Mr. Frank right to the cavalryman's body.

It's time to head back 'n tell Momma I found a Yankee, but it ain't the one I went lookin' for. Ben, waitin' by the rail fence brays when he sees Tater. The seine 'minds me to try'n catch some fish 'fore goin' back to the cabin but...

"Wait, Ben, will Momma 'member it takes two people to drag a seine through the creek?" As I shoulder the seinin' net, a red tail hawk comes outta nowhere 'n screeches at me.

"I reckon he wants me to catch 'im some fish too." The hawk screeches 'gain 'n flies towards the cabin.

"What'd that hawk say, Ben? Did Mr. Frank come back? Let's make haste 'n see."

Tater races 'head 'n Ben trots 'long by me. In the barn I look for Mr. Frank in every stall 'fore climbin' to the hayloft. The spot 'o hope I had for findin' my injun *niji* melts in the hot dusty loft. Like always, I drop a bunch o' peanuts through the hole 'n climb down. The spirit stick's still in the cart holdin' the rest o' Mr.

Frank's secrets. I tuck it under my arm with the net 'n take 'em to the back stoop.

"I don't see no fish," Momma says, tryin' to hold back a laugh. "I figgered you done found a way to seine the creek by yo'self—I reckon'd you'd have a mess 'o perch by now." Then she breaks out laughin'.

"Yessum...I mean no'm. But I found the cavalryman that washed down the creek."

"Lordy, chile, what you done with 'im?"

"Ain't done nothin'. Mr. Frank found 'im first 'n hauled 'im 'way from the creek in my cart. He buried 'im 'side the old cotton field."

Momma's eyes git wider. "You done seen Mr. Frank?"

"No'm, but I read the signs jist like he tol' me."

"But you can't read, Joe."

"Mr. Frank said readin's more'n jist cipherin' words." I grin 'n hold my chin up.

Momma smiles 'n shakes 'er head, "One day you gonna read words 'n then you'll be smart as you think you are." She heads to the kitchen cluckin' 'er tongue like she don't know what to do 'bout me. I wander out to the springhouse with a splinter o' hope Mr. Frank ain't really gone. I throw the spirit stick on the trail by the poplar roots, hopin' to draw 'im outta hidin'. Doves fly outta the bushes, then everythin' gets quiet. The stick jist lays there like a reg'lar limb that broke off 'n fell.

Knowin' Mr. Frank's gone for good makes it hard to swallow my own spit. It's easy to reckon why he couldn't stay 'round here, but my heart ain't ready for 'im to go. I pick up the spirit stick 'n draw back to throw it far off in the woods. Somethin' tells me not to do it. I look at the feathers wavin' in the breeze. Mr. Frank's tellin' me somethin', but what? I go back to the cabin 'n wait.

The next day Momma wakes me 'fore ol' red rooster crows. "Make haste, Joe. We goin' up to Oglethorpe."

"But, Momma, I got peanuts ready to roast in the pot." She puts 'er hands on 'er hips 'n gives me a look—the kind that changes my plans.

"Yessum."

Soon's we eat breakfast I hitch the mules 'n git Tater in the wagon. Momma comes out wearin' 'er best dress, 'n ain't no apron over it. She ties a purty blue ribbon 'round 'er straw hat to make it look goin'-to-town fancy. After tuckin' a basket o' vittles under the seat, I give 'er a hand up 'n she sees 'em—my bare feet.

"Lordy, chile, you go get yo' shoes. We goin' to town."

On the way to Oglethorpe Momma tells me how to act. "All we gonna do is buy some necessaries 'n then head back to the farm. Don't ask fo' nothin', and don't take nothin' from folk you don't know. Don't answer no questions, jist keep yo' eyes on the ground." She says it over 'n over like I ain't never been to town. Maybe she don't 'member Massa Carter brung me to town one winter 'n bought me them shoes I outgrowed last year.

The sun's high when we git to the edge o' town. Ain't many wagons on the main road in the heat o' day. I pull on the reins to stop where Momma points. She fixes 'er hat 'n steps off the wagon. She ain't been in the store more'n two shakes of a squirrel's tail 'til she stalks right back out wearin' 'er mad face.

"Follow me up the road, Joe." She jerks 'round 'n heads up the road. I loosen the reins 'n the mules step in b'hind Momma. She goes in the store past the blacksmith shop. A man wearin' a' apron comes out, waves at me 'n goes back inside. It's the same man that sold Massa Carter my shoes. I wait with the team at the waterin' trough. After a spell, Momma comes outta the store with 'er arms full o' goods, followed by the man in the apron. She sets 'em in the wagon, then goes back inside, but the man stays 'n hands me a twist o' molasses candy.

"Here you go, son." I shake my head like Momma tol' me, my mouth waterin' for the candy. "Go on, take it, won't cost you a penny." My warm fingers stick to the candy.

"Looks like you grew out of the shoes I sold you. Where'd you buy those?" I lick the sweet candy, starin' at the wagon bed. "Don't make shoes like they used to. These days the war's taken all the good cowhides for soldiers' boots." White men don't talk nice to me much, so I ain't sure what to say.

Momma comes out with 'nother load o' goods. Then the man looks up at me 'n asks, "Son, have you heard from your daddy lately?" I don't understand—is this sutler playin' with my mind? Don't he know I ain't got no daddy? I drop my head like Momma tol' me.

Momma butts in, "Massa Green, I reckon I'll take 'nother look at that bolt o' gingham, suh." He follows Momma to the door, but then changes her mind 'n climbs in the wagon. "Git movin', Joe, daylight's a wastin'."

Mr. Green waves 'n hollers from the porch, "Give my best to Major Carter." I stuff the rest o' the candy in my mouth 'n snap the reins with sticky fingers.

"Lord a'mighty, d'liver us from this place o' sin 'n shame 'fore my soul turns sour," Momma prays. As we pass back by the first store, a frownin' man stands out front with 'is arms folded, starin' holes through us.

Momma jist lifts 'er chin high 'n prays, "Lord, I'm askin' you to fo'give that man fo' the way he treats colored folk 'cause I sho' can't...not if I live a thousand years." On down the road, Momma quits huffin' 'n puffin'.

"What'd that store man do to git you riled up?"

Momma bites 'er lip 'n shakes 'er head like she ain't gonna tell me nothin'. Then she looks at me 'n takes a deep breath. "I reckon it ain't no use 'n hidin' you from all the meanness in this world. That devil's disciple tol' me Massa Carter's credit ain't good no mo'. I tol' him I come with cash money. He tol' me...in such words...that slave money ain't no good neither."

"So you got mad 'n walked outta his store?"

"He said some mo' words the Lord don't 'llow my tongue to repeat."

I reckon I done heard them words at the camp. But, I might not hear 'em no more now that Corporal Tolliver can't talk. We rattle 'n bump on down Oglethorpe Road a good ways 'fore I say anythin' else.

"The sutler at the other store was mighty nice wan't he, Momma."

"Umm huh, 'cept the sun's done teched 'is mind so bad it's set his tongue a waggin' like a crow in the corn field."

"Yessum." Listenin' to Momma, I reckon she don't want me makin' no sense outta what Massa Green said. But, I wonder why'd he call Massa Carter my daddy. All the way back to Anderson Station, I think 'bout all the times Massa Carter took pains to show me things, all the times he 'splained things to me, things he never done with other field hands' chillun. I liked bein' with Massa Carter, but why'd he like bein' with me?

15

We git back from Oglethorpe with jist 'nough daylight left to do the chores. When Momma sees the big house, she draws a deep breath 'n leans forward shadin' her eyes.

"Somebody's done come," she says. My belly turns a flip, reckon trouble's found us again. I untie Tater so he can jump off the wagon 'n run 'head. He barks once, then settles down like he knows 'em. Gittin' closer, we see Massa Carter's carriage an' 'is bay horse at the hitchin' post.

"Lordy," Momma cries. She jumps off the wagon 'n takes off runnin' to the big house. A man comes to the front porch 'n he ain't Massa Carter; it's Missy Carter's daddy from Macon. Momma slows to a walk while I drive the team 'round the house to the cabin. I ain't wantin' to hear what that man's got on 'is mind; sho'ly hankerin' to make me a field hand.

I back the wagon into the shade o' the barn. The goods'll keep 'til I find out what Mr. Jim's up to. After unhitchin' the mules, I duck into the cellar o' the big house 'n head to the kitchen where I can heah Momma 'n Mr. Jim talkin'. What they sayin'? I can't make it out, so I sneak to the front room to heah 'em better. Momma's whimperin'.

"Please, Massa Jim, don't take my boy." That's all I need to heah. I turn tail, sneak out through the cellar 'n head back to the cabin. I got no time to think 'bout goin' to Macon with that man 'n leavin' Momma by herself. She needs me.

I stop at the well for a quick drink. 'Fore I put the gourd to my lips, the spirit stick falls over on the porch where I leaned it 'gainst the wall. Is this a sign from Mr. Frank? I pick up the stick 'n hold it over my head.

"Mr. Frank, send yo' spirit to git me outta trouble." Closin' my eyes tight, I rub my fingers up 'n down the spirit stick. "*Manitos,* where can I go now?" I pray, hopin' I called the injun spirits by the right name. Voices from the front yard break the silence; I gotta go. The trail behind the springhouse is my only way out. Crouchin' low, I head for the openin' in the woods' hopin' Tater don't follow 'n give me 'way. Slippin' 'n slidin' all the way down the steep hill, I come to the ford. The creek runs shallow now, so I make my way 'long the sandy bed, walkin' backwards, brushin' over my tracks with a gum limb. Coverin' my tracks slows me down, so I take off my shoes 'n walk in the creek, a trick Mr. Frank showed me to throw bloodhounds off my trail 'n Tater too, if he comes after me. I reckon Mr. Jim won't call for Mr. Turner's bloodhounds, but I jist don't know 'bout that.

A little ways ahead is Mr. Frank's shelter where we hunkered down in the storm. I cup my hands 'n blow 'tween my thumbs, makin' a dove's call to see if anythin' made a nest in the shelter. Nothin' answers so I look inside. It's empty. I plop down on the dry pine straw to catch my breath 'n think. It's a good place to wait 'n listen for Mr. Jim in case he tracks me down.

The sun takes forever to set. I reckon I got nothin' to do but think 'n listen. Dark comes faster when I got chores to git done. For somethin' to do, I push the spirit stick 'tween pine branches in the shelter so its feathers hang down. The feathers brush 'gainst my face in the breeze 'n makes me wonder 'bout Mr. Frank. Is he safe or did the guards find 'im and send 'im back to the stockade? What would he tell me to do? I try hard to think like Mr. Frank, like a' injun.

He'd say, "Listen to the sounds, look for signs, let yourself be part of everything around you." I jist don't know how to do it. I need help.

The sun finally drops b'hind the tall pines. I cross my legs like Mr. Frank 'n watch the shadows move 'cross the clearin' 'tween me 'n the creek. Somethin' moves in the brush. A rabbit creeps out 'n nibbles on grass 'n it makes me hungry. Somethin' rustles 'n scares the rabbit back in the brush. A doe steps outta the shadows to graze in the clearin'. She lifts 'er head, sniffs the air 'n keeps on grazin'. Then the rabbit comes back out to eat. It's a mystery why two animals that always run from me are now eatin' supper while I watch. I don't wanna scare 'em away, so I set still as a rock. A shadow moves down a gum tree by the creek. I can't make out what's headin' my way 'til it gets closer. It's a coon, walkin' right up to where I can jist 'bout touch it. It sniffs the air, looks at me 'n then wanders on b'hind the shelter, actin' jist like I'm s'posed to be here.

I watch the animals feedin' 'til daylight fades. The woods come to life 'round me with clickin' crickets 'n whinin' katydids, a lot louder than I ever heard from the front porch. Skeeters buzz 'round my head, bullfrogs croak in the marsh by the creek, owls start hootin' back 'n forth, 'n a bobcat's scream sends chills down my back. I'm a settin' here in the dark with critters that I can't see, all goin' 'bout their bi'ness. Why ain't I 'fraid? It's like bein' here with Mr. Frank. I wait for the moon to come up so I can see my way back to the cabin.

My legs ache from settin' cross-legged, so I stretch out on the straw. I reach up in the dark to touch the spirit stick, to be sure it's still with me.

"*Manitos*, what should I do? Will Mr. Jim spend the night in the big house waitin' to take me to Macon in the mornin'?" After a while, more'n half a moon peeps through the gum trees over the creek. It flushes out more night critters that start movin' all 'round me. Somethin' splashes in the creek, a fox barks, a whippoorwill cuts through the night air with its sharp call. I figger these critters're tellin' me, "Don't leave, stay in the woods 'til mornin'." I pull the spirit stick close to my chest 'n settle in for the night. I'd swap this stick for Tater right now.

Time passes slow as cold molasses 'n plays tricks with my head. Am I sleepin' or wakin'? I can't tell. Mr. Frank comes to the shelter, 'n next minute he ain't there, or is he? My eyes open wide but I can't see much. Sleep comes over me 'til a loud crash in the brush 'hind the shelter scares me awake again—is it a bear, a wild hog, or a prison guard? I take a deep breath, tryin' to git a' hold o' myself 'n git rid o' the shakes. I have trouble gittin' back to sleep.

Sun up comes bringin' the daylight I been longin' to see. Night noises give way to chirpin' birds. A deer, a rabbit 'n some squirrels come out to eat breakfast. A woodpecker taps overhead. My stomach growls for food 'n water. I crawl outta the shelter. Kneelin' by the creek for a drink, my skin draws tight like somebody's watchin' me. I hurry back to the shelter to hide, spookin' the animals back to the brush.

Why ain't Mr. Jim come after me? The rabbit sticks 'is head outta the brush to see if it's safe t' come out. I cross my legs 'n rub my fingers on the spirit stick.

"What's gonna happen to me *Manitos*? Why ain't you showed me what to do?"

I ain't sure if Mr. Jim's waitin' for me to come back to the big house. I gotta hide here to give 'im time to give up 'n head back to Macon. My stomach keeps on growlin', my mouth's dry 'n my head's in a fog. The sun lights up the clearin' but nothin's movin' 'cept the creek washin' over rocks.

Voices start runnin' through my head.

I hear Momma sayin', *Don't take my boy.*

Then I hear Mr. Frank sayin', *I'll take your boy to a shelter and leave him without food 'til he finds his purpose on earth.*

Then Momma fusses at Mr. Frank for takin' me off, but she's got it mixed up. It's Mr. Jim—he's the one who made me run to the woods. The fussin' keeps up in my mind 'til I get weary, curl up on the pine straw 'n catch up on lost sleep.

Boom!

Thunder jolts me from my dreams. Don't see no clouds in the sky.

Boom!

It's comin' from the camp. It ain't thunder, it's Capt'n Wirtz shootin' off 'is cannons to scare prisoners outta tryin' to 'scape. 'Spite o' somebody might be watchin', I ease over to the creek for a drink, too thirsty to care 'bout it. I suck water from my cupped hands 'n then splash it on my face to git waked up good.

Back in the shelter, I figger on stayin' hid 'least 'til sundown. My empty belly don't quit rumbin'; it starts playin' tricks with my mind. Corporal Tolliver screams loud at me, *Half-breed you made me git killed. I'm a comin' outta my grave and skin you like a rabbit.* I shake my head good 'n look 'cross the creek to make sure 'is ghost ain't risin' up from the dead to git me. That grave's on the ridge 'cross the creek, but my bones tell me it's too close.

Momma's done got in my mind 'gain sayin', *Stay hid, Joe. Ain't nobody gonna take you 'way from me.* Do I see 'er standin' in the clearin', huggin' 'er body as she talks or am I goin' crazy? Maybe fillin' my belly with blackberries'll shake off this spell. After crawlin' outta the shelter I stand up 'n my legs creak 'n buckle from settin' cross-legged a long time.

Mr. Frank's voice shoots through my mind like a sharp arrow. *Don't eat 'til you know your purpose, Joe. Let the Manitos be your guide. Listen...listen...listen...* A quick stretch gets the kinks outta my arms 'n legs 'fore I crawl back in the shelter. All the other voices go 'way—I hear my own voice, echoin' like from down in a well. *Who is Joe the peanut boy, Goober Joe, the boy without a real name?* I hear nothin' but questions, no answers.

"Help me spirit stick, help me snuff out the voices in my head. Give me a name 'sides Goober, a good name, a name that fits with Joe."

As the sun drops lower, somethin' takes hold o' me 'n won't let me leave the shelter. I have to stay...I have to stay 'til it turns me loose. My belly's still empty, my mouth still dry, my legs still hurt; my brain whirls round 'n round inside my head like feathers in the wind, like itchin' in places I can't scratch.

Was it Mr. Frank's spirit that led me out here to be alone? A feelin' comes over me like I b'long here in the woods. That echo inside me says, *Stay in the shelter another night, Joe. You are not alone. Stay hungry 'til you know who you are.*

The rabbit 'n the deer come out to feed 'gain as the sun goes down, still not afraid o' me. A red tail hawk on a low pine limb waits for some critter to stray too far from cover.

"Hey, Mr. Hawk, you know which way Mr. Frank went?" The woods get quiet at the sound o' my voice, but 'fore long the crickets, katydids 'n frogs tune up to sing. The hawk sets on the limb 'til it turns into a shadow watchin' over me in the dark.

My second night in the shelter starts out the same, but soon things change. A mist crawls over the creek bank 'n the moon gits a ring 'round it. The voices in my head run outta things to say. I fall asleep.

"Joe."

Who's callin' my name? I can barely open my eyes 'cause they're wet with tears I don't 'member sheddin'. Clearin' my eyes don't help 'cause the fog's too thick to see through. Is it Mr. Jim? I ain't gonna answer 'im.

"Joe, I come here to help you." It don't sound like Mr. Jim. I push up 'n wipe my eyes 'gain, searchin' for the man out there in the fog. The moon gives jist 'nough light to make out a shadow in the clearin'.

"Tell me your dreams, Joe."

I try to ask the man 'is name, but that shadow's done tied up my tongue. I can only do dream talk. "Yessuh, I dreamed 'bout…"

"Joe, don't call me 'sir'."

"Niji!"

Everythin' gits quiet 'cept the bubblin' o' the creek.

"Go on."

"My dreams're mixed up. I'm a little boy, playin' hoops with the kids at Camp Sumter. They tell me to take off my shoes.

Then they start laughin' at my feet. 'You got black feet—we can't play with you.' I look down 'n see my feet turned black. I pull up the bottom o' my britches 'n my legs're black too. I run all the way back to the big house to play with the field hands' kids. They laugh at me sayin' they ain't 'llowed to play with a white face kid." I wait for the shadow to tell me 'bout my dream.

"Go on."

I wanna tell 'im dreams ain't easy to recall, but the words don't come out. After a bit, the hawk dream comes to mind.

"I dream I turn into a hawk, a red tail hawk with a sharp beak. I fly off to the camp to peck out the eyes of all the kids that ever made fun o' me. As I fly over the stockade another hawk digs outta the grave ditch 'n flys 'long with me. He says, 'Where you goin' Goober Hawk?' I tell 'im what I wanna do to the camp kids. He says, 'Won't do no good.' I ask 'im why 'n he says, 'They'll see you the same way even with their eyes put out.' I ask 'im how he knows so much. He says, 'The higher you fly, the more you see.' Then he takes off flyin' to the sun."

Again I wait, but the shadow says, "Go on."

One more dream waits, but it's too scary to tell. I try to fall asleep 'gain, but sleep won't come.

"I wait," the shadow says.

Takin' a deep breath brings courage—so, I tell the last dream.

"One day the Union cavalry rides to Camp Sumter. 'Stead o' fightin', all the guards lay down their guns 'n jist start home. The bluecoats pull down the stockade gate 'n load the prisoners on a train. When the train pulls out 'n the cavalry leaves, dead soldiers march out o' Union grave ditches, nothin' but skin 'n bones. They march over to Mr. Dukes' store like they wanna trade for somethin' to eat. But all they have to sell is their names. I try to trade a token for a dead soldier's name, but Momma slaps my hand 'n says, 'You can't buy a dead white man's name.' I find a black soldier tryin' to sell his name, but Momma slaps my hand 'gain. 'You can't buy a dead black man's name.' I start cryin' 'n

the dead soldiers march back to their grave ditches singin',
'Goober Joe ain't no name, if a pig had it, he'd be 'shamed.'
That's when you woke me up callin' my name."

"You're a good boy, Joe and you will grow to become a good
man. Fasting purifies your soul and dreams sharpen your vision.
From now on you will hunger for the knowledge of the creatures
and thirst for the wisdom of the earth." The fog starts to swirl
'round the fuzzy shadow.

"Wait! What 'bout my dreams? Tell me what they mean."

A hollow voice echoes from the fog before it fades away,
"Your vision quest is over, Joe. Now look deep inside yourself to
find the answers to your questions, and your new name…"

The fog thickens 'n swallows the shadow. The moon shrinks
to a pale glow, then disappears. Darkness—then sleep wraps
'round my weary mind.

16

Somethin' wet laps 'gainst my face wakin' me up.

"Tater! What you doin' here?" My eyes fight the mornin' sun pokin' through the pines. The fog's lifted 'n left a ghost trail over the creek bed. I roll outta the shelter, barely able to move my arms 'n legs. Tater's barkin' wantin' to play. "Hush, Tater, I'm tryin' to hide."

"Joe, O Joe!" Momma's voice sings out from 'cross the creek. I shade my eyes 'n look to see if she brought Mr. Jim with 'er. "Joe, where you at?"

Ain't nobody with 'er. "Heah, Momma, 'cross the creek."

"Lordy, Joe, come out so I can see you. You done scared the life outta me." Tater whines 'n watches me wobble to my feet like I'm gittin' old. I wave to Momma though my arm feels like it might break off. "You hurtin' chile?" she hollers.

I shake my head no 'n stumble over to the creek. I start to step in the water, but then turn back to get my shoes 'n spirit stick. I cross the creek 'n Momma smothers me with hugs 'fore she turns to scoldin' me.

"Chile, you could a drowned or you could a got killed by a bear or bit by a rattlesnake. What if you'd o' starved to death?" Momma runs outta breath caterwaulin' 'bout things I ain't worried 'bout—'cept starvin'.

"Yessum, 'n I could a got hauled off to Macon to work for Mr. Jim."

Momma's mouth falls open. "Massa Jim? Did he make you run off down heah?"

"Yessum."

"You oughta know I'd put up a fight 'fore I'd let you go. C'mon, let's git you back to the cabin 'n git some vittles in you. Then we gonna talk a while."

"Mr. Jim?"

"He stayed the night in the big house. Next mornin' he figgered you done run away for good. So he went on back to Macon after I fixed 'im some breakfast. I don't know what got hold o' you, to scare yo' momma like this, chile, I jist don't know." Momma walks close to me, holdin' my overall galluses like I'm gonna turn tail 'n run off 'gain.

"I heard 'im say he'd take me back to Macon with 'im."

"Um huh," Momma says, shakin' 'er head. "We might both go up to Macon to help pick cotton come fall." She don't say what made 'er change her mind 'bout helpin' Mr. Jim. She follows me through the cornfield, still holdin' onto my overalls. A red tail hawk hovers overhead not makin' a sound. I grip the spirit stick 'n walk tall, wonderin' if Momma can tell me what my dreams mean.

"Joe, come on to the kitchen while I cook you somethin'."

I can't jist set 'n watch Momma fix breakfast, I gotta do somethin' 'sides wait. "I'll take care o' the livestock 'n gather eggs 'til it's ready."

"You too weak to work right now, 'sides I got things to talk 'bout." Her tone o' voice makes me squirm in the chair. It ain't like Momma to let me put off mornin' chores. The fatback crackles in the skillet; its sweet burnt smell reaches my nose. Now I know how much I miss eatin'. "Heah, drink some milk first so yo' stomach'll get used to food 'gain." She pours sweet milk into my jar. "Drink it slow."

"Yessum."

She goes back to the stove with 'er questions poppin' like green wood on a hot fire. "Were you scared? You see any snakes? Did you git any sleep?" On 'n on she goes, not stoppin' fo' my answers, like she really don't wanna to know 'bout me bein' in the woods. I'll put off tellin' 'er my dreams 'til a better time.

She piles up hoecakes 'n fat back on a plate 'n watches me. I pour a circle o' sorghum on top 'n start eatin'. Momma don't eat, jist pulls up a chair 'n watches me eat. I can tell by 'er raised eyebrows 'n crinkly grin that she's glad I'm back 'n dyin' to tell me somethin'.

"Joe, Massa Jim brought word from Massa Carter." She pulls a paper outta 'er apron pocket 'n spreads it on the table. Pressin' 'er fingers over the paper, Momma wiggles 'er shoulders 'n head like she jist found a gold mine. "Massa Carter's done come back to Macon, lettin' 'is legs heal up."

Now I know why Momma changed 'er mind 'bout goin' to Macon to pick cotton.

She goes on, "The army's gonna send all the bluecoats in the stockade back up north 'n swap 'em for Confederate prisoners. Soon's they clear out the prison, Massa Carter gonna bring Missy Carter 'n the girls back to the big house to live."

"How's Massa Carter gonna work the farm with both 'is legs shot off?"

Momma bristles. "Lordy, Lordy, that Mr. Dukes don't know truth if it's hangin' on 'is scalp like a tick. Massa Jim tol' me Massa Carter took Yankee shot in both legs, but he can walk 'n ride a horse like the next man. They ain't never cut off 'is legs, no suh, he's comin' back whole."

Momma's eyes get brighter, she talks 'bout Massa Carter comin' home. Figger I oughta be happy like Momma, but I ain't. Maybe it's 'cause I'm weak from them two days with nothin' t'eat. Momma notices.

"Ain't that good news, chile, ain't you happy 'bout Massa Carter?"

"Yessum." I finish soppin' up the last o' the sorghum syrup with the hoecake 'n stuff it in my mouth.

"Then why's yo' chin 'bout to fall in yo' plate?"

"I'm jist wonderin'…" Momma leans over the table like she wants to hear what I say. "When Massa Carter gits back, who gonna work this big 'ol farm 'sides me 'n him?"

"Well, I ain't got to that part yet. It's writ down," she irons the paper flat with her fingers, "right heah. When the war's over, Massa Carter's gonna give field hands part o' this land, if they come back 'n work on shares. Ain't that somethin', Joe, a place o' they own?"

"Yessum, but what we gonna do?"

"This paper says we can stay in this cabin for good."

"And what we gonna swap Massa Carter for the cabin?" Momma's face wrinkles up 'n she leans back in 'er chair starin' at the paper on the table.

"You go on to the barn 'n let the livestock out to pasture. Then build me fire under the wash pot so I can wash them filthy overalls." I didn't mean to throw water on Momma's glowin' coals. A lot more questions come to mind, but she's done talkin' for now. After turnin' the cows 'n mules out, I take a' ear o' dried corn to Ben. He sets in 'is stall nibblin' on it while I talk to 'im.

"Well, Mr. Ben, you glad I came back?" Tater whines when I talk to Ben, jealous I reckon. "Looks like our peanut tradin' days'll soon be over. Prisoners're goin' home 'n Camp Sumter's gonna shut down. I won't have time to roast 'n boil peanuts nohow. Massa Carter gonna put me to work with the field hands." Ben finishes gnawin' the corncob 'n kicks the gate, wantin' out. I open it 'n he trots to the pasture 'fore I even scratch 'is ears. My mind's buzzin' with questions anyway. I take my spirit stick up to the loft to set 'n think.

My legs still ache but I ease down cross-legged on Mr. Frank's nest o' hay. I close my eyes 'n dream 'bout flyin', not like eagles or hawks, but fast like hummingbirds. I fly outta the loft 'n head north lookin' for Mr. Frank. Soon's I leave the farm, a flock o' bigger birds come after me. 'Fraid they'll eat me, I turn back. I open my eyes, knowin' I ain't never gonna be a bird like Mr. Frank. Can't never be Goober Joe no more neither.

I climb down from the loft 'n split kindlin' for the fire. The ax slices through the lightered pine strikin' my nose with the fresh sweet smell o' turpentine. I lay the split sticks under the big iron pot 'n cover 'em with bigger sticks o' hickory 'n oak. Momma lights the fire 'n we watch the white smoke curl up jist b'fore the red 'n orange flames start lickin' the sides o' the big black iron pot.

"Somethin' I forgot to tell you a while ago, Joe. You been grievin' 'cause you ain't got no family name. I think it's fittin' we git you a name, a good name like you want."

My heart jumps 'n thumps faster. It works! The vision quest works! Momma's gonna give me a name—a real name, 'fore I even tell 'er 'bout my dreams.

"Yessum, yessum," I holler, dancin' up 'n down 'round the fire.

"When Massa Carter comes back to the farm, I'm gonna ask 'im to give me 'n you his name." She juts out 'er chin, "Della Carter 'n 'er boy Joe Carter. Won't that be fine?"

"Yessum."

I quit jumpin' 'round. She pokes the fire under the pot, grins big 'n starts hummin'. I turn my back so she don't see my face.

"Now take off yo' clothes so I can wash 'em." I shed my overalls 'n shirt 'n hand 'em to Momma. "Everythin' outta yo' pockets?" she asks. I reach in a pocket for my knife 'n feel somethin' else—the wad of *kinikinic* Mr. Frank gave me to make us *nijis*. I run to the cabin for some clean clothes, squeezin' the tobacco tight in my fist.

I stand jist 'bout buck naked in the cabin lookin' at my white skin an' sayin' over 'n over, "Joe Carter...Joe Carter...Joe Carter." I open my hand to sniff the tobacco. The name jist don't fit right. It jist don't fit with the rich smell o' *kinikinic*. Carter...it hangs heavy on my tongue every time I say it. I slip on clean overalls, not botherin' with a shirt, 'n go to fetch the spirit stick.

Momma's too busy washin' to notice me slippin' back to the barn. Holdin' the stick tight, I head to the creek through the pasture, to keep Tater from followin' me. The whistle at the depot wails three times. The train's fixin' to haul prisoners 'way from Anderson Station. Changes are a comin', ain't got much time to get ready.

I run fast 'til I see the rocks piled on Corporal Tolliver's grave. I slow to a walk, not outta fear, but respect for the dead. Even though he was mean to me, I never wished for 'im to git killed. Somethin' leads me 'cross the creek 'n up the stream to the shelter. I fall to my knees on the pine straw 'n stare at the back wall a long time. Then I close my eyes 'n listen, hopin' the *Manitos* gonna speak to me 'n give me a name, somethin' 'sides Carter.

Silence.

Inside the shelter, I open my eyes 'n wave the spirit stick.

"Oh *Manitos,* I had three dreams here last night. Tell me what they mean. I have no one else to tell my dreams to." The bubblin' creek's the only thing that answers me. I get to my feet 'n look 'round for any sign o' Mr. Frank's spirit. The limb where the red tail hawk stood watch over me's now empty. The sky's clear, ain't even no crows flyin' through the pines. My hand aches from squeezin' the tobacco too tight. I loosen my fist 'n look at the damp tobacco. I take a pinch, scatter it on the pine straw 'n try to use a heavy voice like Mr. Frank's.

"I bring you *kinikinic* for givin' me a good shelter. I am part o' this place, *niji* to all that live here." I put the rest o' the tobacco in my pocket 'n lift the spirit stick high. "Mr. Frank, you're my *niji* too." I lower the stick 'n head back to the cabin.

Walkin' 'tween the cornrows, I start to feel as tall as the brown stalks. With every step, the soft dirt under my bare feet springs back, makin' me feel lighter 'n lighter. A red tail hawk flies overhead 'n let's out a long screech at me.

"Mr. Frank," I holler, but the hawk flies over the pasture without answerin'.

Momma's out back hangin' clothes on the line. Tater runs to meet me. "Where you been, chile? I been callin' you a while."

"Thinkin'."

"Well, you got mo' to do 'round heah than jist thinkin'. Time fo' mo' stove wood 'n I need a bucket o' water 'n some sweet potatoes. Don't forgit to throw some hay down from the loft 'n clean out the milkin' stalls."

"Yessum."

All the while I'm workin' my dreams bounce 'round in my head like they wanna git loose. I can tell Momma my dreams, but that ain't all—I gotta tell 'er I ain't gonna take Massa Carter's name for my own. She was so proud when she told me 'bout it; she ain't gonna like what I say. Mr. Frank says a boy's daddy or granddaddy's s'posed to come up with 'is new name, but it ain't gonna happen fo' me. I gotta find my own name, but ain't no name come to me yet. I try to think o' bird names, but nothin' sounds right—*Joe Hawk; Joe Eagle; Joe Crow; Joe Woodpecker,* so I give up worryin' 'bout a name 'n dig up a mess o' sweet potatoes 'n take 'em to the kitchen.

"Might as well stay 'n eat somethin' 'fore goin' back out in the scorchin' sun," Momma says, still tryin' to fill me up.

"Yessum." I spread the yams out on the back stoop in the sun to cure. Momma sets a plate o' cornbread 'n peas on the table. "Ain't you gonna eat, too?" I ask.

"You go on while I'm gittin' this corn ready to make hominy. Good thing the guards didn't find these ears under the back stoop." I eat a mite slow, hopin' to catch 'er in a listenin' mood. She twists the ears o' dried yellow corn, scatterin' the kernels in the dishpan. She stops to wipe the sweat off 'er face.

"Momma, I had a dream last night."

"Umm huh."

"I dreamed I had black feet 'n a white face 'n nobody would play with me."

"Umm huh."

"Then I dreamed I turned into a hawk 'n went to peck out the eyes o' the kids that wouldn't play with me."

"Umm huh."

"Then I dreamed Union prisoners, white ones 'n colored ones rose outta the grave ditches wantin' to sell me their names."

"Umm huh, sounds like bein' hungry mixed up yo' mind, chile," Momma laughs. She comes to the table to wash the corn.

I take a deep breath 'n say, "Momma, I ain't gonna take Massa Carter's name. I ain't gonna be Joe Carter."

Momma pushes the dishpan back 'n leans towards me, 'er face full o' frown. "What you sayin', chile? You tol' me you want 'nother name."

"But you tol' me to pay no 'tention to names other folk give me."

"Um huh…not even yo' momma?"

"You done give me one name I'm proud to bear. But it's time to let my dreams turn loose the man inside me."

"Umm huh."

I push back from the table 'n stand up straight, takin' a deep breath so I can use my man's voice. Momma jerks 'er head back like she don't know me nomore.

"From now on you can call me *JOE FRANK.*"

I don't know how Mr. Frank's name came outta my mouth. It jist popped out—like it'd been hidin' under my tongue the whole time.

Momma runs her eyes up 'n down, like she wants me to take back what I jist called myself. I stand strong, takin' my first breath as a real man with a real name, wonderin' what Momma's gonna say. After a while, a tiny smile creeps 'cross 'er face 'n grows to a big one, showin' 'er shinin' white teeth. Then she breaks out in a deep head-shakin' laugh.

"Uh uh uh, chile," Momma gits up 'n wraps 'er long skinny arms 'round me. "I reckon I gotta quit callin' you *chile.* I reckon little Joe done outgrowed 'is britches. Don't you reckon that's so, *Mister Joe Frank*?"

"Yessum."

The End

Ojibwe/French Vocabulary

Anishinabe—Original man
Assema—tobacco
Black robes—French Jesuit priests
Bois brulé—(burnt wood) French fur traders' term for a person
    with French and Ojibwe blood.
Boozhoo—Ojibwe greeting
Chippewa—Another name for Ojibwe
Gitchi Gami—The Great Water (Lake Superior)
Gitchi Manito—Great Spirit or Creator
Kinikinic—Ceremonial tobacco mixed with willow bark
Manitos—Spirits
Manomin—Wild rice
Métis—French term for a mixed race Ojibwe/French person
Midewiwin—The Grand Medicine Society of Spiritual Healers
Meegwich—Goodbye
Mishomis—Grandfather
Niji—Friend or brother
Wigiwam—Ojibwe dwelling made of natural materials

Civil War Vocabulary

Bluecoats—common name for Union soldiers
Confed—common name for Confederate or Confederacy
Croaker sack—large burlap bag
Dead line—a forbidden area along the interior stockade wall
Fresh fish—slang term for new Union prisoners
Goobers—peanuts
Johnny Rebs—Confederate soldiers
Pigeon roosts—guard stations along the stockade wall
Shebangs—makeshift shelters made by prisoners
Sutler—merchant or peddler
Tokens—coins made of pressed cardboard used as money

www.ingramcontent.com/pod-product-compliance
Lightning Source LLC
Chambersburg PA
CBHW022152080426
42734CB00006B/398